NANCIE ATWELL & ANNE ATWELL MERKEL

The Reading Zone

How to Help Kids Become Passionate, Skilled, Habitual, Critical Readers

Second Edition

SCHOLASTIC

Every Child a Reader by Helene Coffin. Copyright © 2009 by Helene Coffin. Published by Scholastic Inc.
"Miracles" from *Leaves of Grass*, Second Edition by Walt Whitman. Originally published by Fowler and Wells, 1856.
"shreds of grass" is an unpublished student poem, used by permission.

Publisher: Lois Bridges
Editor-in-Chief: Raymond Coutu
Development/Production Editor: Danny Miller
Editorial Director: Sarah Longhi
Art Director/Cover Designer: Brian J. LaRossa
Interior Designer: Jaime Lucero
Photographer: Erin Moore/Mercy Street Studios

Portions previously published in *The Reading Zone*, First Edition, copyright © 2007 by Nancie Atwell.

Copyright © 2016 by Nancie Atwell and Anne Atwell Merkel.

All rights reserved.   Published by Scholastic Inc.   Printed in the USA.

ISBN-13: 978-0-545-94874-6

for Thomas Newkirk,
our Michel de Montaigne

The days that make us happy

make us wise.

—John Masefield

Table of Contents

Acknowledgments

Many people had a hand in the second edition of *The Reading Zone*. Special thanks go to the extraordinary reading teachers at the Center for Teaching and Learning (CTL), Caroline Bond, Ted DeMille, Jill Cotta, Glenn Powers, and Helene Coffin, our Kindergarten Teacher Emerita. They are a heroic faculty, dedicated head, heart, and soul to the personal artists they nurture. Thank you, too, to the personal artists: the years of students from whom we've learned about classroom conditions that make reading easy and readers happy.

We're grateful to Tom Newkirk and Dorothy Stephens for insights at critical junctures; to Shelley Harwayne for her eloquent foreword; and to Richard Allington, Pam Allyn, Alfie Kohn, Stephen Krashen, and Alfred Tatum for their ideas about how our nation might create a sturdy, vibrant reading zone for all of its children.

We're also grateful to Danny Miller, production editor/manager of this book, for the smart, engaged, efficient coordination of its publication; to Jaime Lucero, who designed the elegant layout; to Suzanne Akceylon, who sorted out the references; to Erin Moore for photographs that reveal CTL readers immersed in the zone; and to Kevin Carlson and his film crew for the impeccable videos of middle school readers and their teacher at work.

We can't thank Toby McLeod and Luke Merkel enough for their patience, support by word and deed, and enthusiasm for this project, not to mention the happiness to be found in a shared life among books.

Finally, *The Reading Zone* exists because of its editor, Lois Bridges. Whether an author is a novice or an old pro, her responses are a writer's dream. Her commitment to children, teachers, literacy, and justice is unwavering. We are indebted to her for her vast knowledge, superb editorial assistance, continuous cheerleading, and easy laughter.

Foreword

The writer Nora Ephron suggested that "There's something called the rapture of the deep, and it refers to what happens when a deep-sea diver spends too much time at the bottom of the ocean and can't tell which way is up. When he resurfaces, he's liable to have a condition called the bends, where the body can't adapt to the oxygen levels in the atmosphere. All this happens to me when I resurface from a book."

Nine years ago, I had the privilege of writing the foreword for the first edition of *The Reading Zone*. I described how the book, brimming with expert, practical, and sane advice for helping students enter their own personal reading zones, made me feel the rapture of the deep. This is no less true of the second edition, now co-authored with Nancie's daughter, Anne Atwell Merkel. When Nancie stepped aside in 2013 as middle school English teacher at the Center for Teaching and Learning, Anne stepped in and continued the tradition of informed, responsive instruction.

With eloquence and honesty, Nancie and Anne show us just how remarkable a room filled with young readers can be. With beautifully crafted classroom scenes, student work samples, and pages packed with sensible suggestions, they remind us of what's important in the teaching of reading. More important, they clear the way for other teachers to invite every student to feel the rapture of the deep, enter their own reading zones, and become the kinds of readers we all dream of.

Today, informed by my current teaching experiences in Harlem charter schools, public city elementary schools, and neighboring suburban classrooms, I write with a sense of urgency. Above all are my experiences as a grandmother to a fourth, fifth, sixth, seventh, and ninth grader. My greatest desire is for my grandchildren to always be in classrooms that celebrate reading for pleasure, personal preference, meaningful literary discussions, and authentic writing about reading.

From the very first chapter onward, Nancie and Anne demonstrate how they help students of all ages and backgrounds, with all needs and interests, turn their reading into a personal art. In this beautifully crafted, updated edition, they challenge conventional wisdom about fiction versus nonfiction, close reading, and reading conferences—or, in their more suitable term, "checking-in" with independent readers. In a chapter on writing about reading, Anne reveals the breathtaking level of literary analysis that's possible when we invite student readers to correspond in "letter-essays."

I easily envision *The Reading Zone* becoming the centerpiece of staff room conversations, challenging literacy educators to rethink their goals, redefine their practice, and reestablish their own reading lives. With brilliant simplicity and expertise, Nancie and Anne make reading easy for students and the teaching of reading a thrilling and artistic endeavor.

—*Shelley Harwayne*
AUTHOR/CONSULTANT

CHAPTER ONE

The Personal Art

An experienced personal artist enjoys his current favorite author, George R. R. Martin

I t's a morning in November. Outside, the sky has already turned the peculiar yellow-grey of winter in Maine. Inside my daughter's classroom, under banks of fluorescent lights, Anne's seventh and eighth graders sprawl on beanbags or drape themselves across desktops. They're decked out in the current uniform of American adolescence: leggings and joggers, logo t-shirts, bright Nikes. Anne has just finished scooting among them and whispering a conversation with each boy and girl: "How is it?" or "What do you think so far?" or "What's happening now?" she asks. "Are you happy?" And, always, "What page are you on?" Now she's back in her rocking chair at the front of the classroom, surveying the group with satisfaction. Except for the sound of pages turning, the room is still.

If you had observed these students on any other occasion in their waking lives— say, yesterday, as they tried to organize themselves into teams for touch football and screamed at one another at top volume for the first 10 minutes of their recess—it would be hard to reconcile that noise with this quiet. But here, in reading workshop, it's dead silent because the kids are gone. Each boy and girl has vanished into an invisible world. Each, as we put it at our school, is lost in the reading zone.

Nineteen students are reading 19 different books. Lucas, an eighth grader, laughs to himself as he turns the pages of *Catch-22*, which Anne extolled in a booktalk a few weeks ago along with other antiwar narratives—Vonnegut's *Slaughterhouse-Five*, *Fallen Angels* by Walter Dean Myers, Chris Crowe's novel-in-haiku *Death Coming up the Hill*, and *The Things They Carried* by Tim O'Brien. Lucas's friend Nicco finished the O'Brien yesterday and rated it a nine out of ten; now, at his older brother's suggestion, he's trying Cormac McCarthy's *The Road*. Christian and Sydney are getting their feet wet in nonfiction—David McCullough's *The Wright Brothers* and *The Glass Castle* by Jeanette Walls, respectively. Emma H., Anne's history buff, is poring over *March*, the graphic memoir by John Lewis that Griffin booktalked last week, while Kaleb barely breathes as he nears the end of Andy Weir's *The Martian*. When Jolie, an eighth grader, says she loves *I Am Malala*, I flash back to last fall, when she wouldn't veer from series fiction. Speaking of which, today Emma C., a seventh grader, is caught up in Rick Yancey's *The Fifth Wave*, the first volume in a dystopian series Jolie loved. Griffin, another seventh grader, has lost himself in the recently released third volume, *The Last Star*.

Hope is absorbed in *These Shallow Graves* by Jennifer Donnelly, a new favorite author since Anne recommended Donnelly's *Revolution*, well aware—as is the whole class—of Hope's obsession with all things *Les Misérables*. Next to Hope, Nolan shakes he is laughing so hard at something in David Sedaris's memoir *Me Talk Pretty One Day*. Zoe, who surprised herself with how much she liked the film version of *To Kill a Mockingbird*, is happily surprising herself with Harper Lee. Katie's chipped manicure blends in with the bright cover of Morgan Matson's latest, *The Unexpected Everything*, and at her side, Ella is nearing the cliffhanger ending of Emmy Laybourne's *Sweet*—I can tell because she catches her teacher's eye and mouths the words *Oh my gosh. I know*, Anne mouths back.

Joe, eighth-grade sports maven, is reading a new baseball novel by Carl Deuker. Last year, Joe wrote an essay making the case for youth baseball amidst the rising popularity of lacrosse, so when Anne skimmed a recent *Booklist* and found *Painting the Black*, about a high school catcher, she bought it with Joe in mind and asked if he wanted to preview it for the group. He's 50 pages in and says so far he'd rate it a nine. His partner-in-crime, Sam, is inhaling Andrew Smith's *Winger*, a funny, heartbreaking take on a boy in a boarding school. Next to him, Graham furrows his brow as he puts

"Diddle Diddle Dumpling": A personal artist in a kindergarten workshop

together the contradictory stories told by the alternating narrators in *How It Went Down* by Kekla Magoon. Lacey just finished Ruta Sepetys's most recent historical novel, *Salt to the Sea*, and is adding it to her reading record. And Lexi, who abandoned two novels in quick succession last week, grabbed Sophie Kinsella's *Finding Audrey* after Anne booktalked it today, mostly for Lexi's benefit. So far, she says, so good.

When Anne notices the time, she clears her throat and says, "As you're ready, find a good stopping place, mark your page, and come up for air." One by one her students segue from the stories they've been living in back to the here and now. They yawn and stretch—it can take a physical effort to cross the boundary. And then they're fully themselves again. They yammer at Anne and each other about their books, overstuff their backpacks, forget to put away the beanbags, and slam out of the room to their next class. Tonight they'll read for at least half an hour—that's everyone's homework every night. Tomorrow in school they'll read some more—the next day, too. By June each boy and girl will have finished at least 30 books; a few will read and record more than a hundred titles.

Frequent, Voluminous, and Self-Selected

The annual average for a class of seventh and eighth graders at our school, the Center for Teaching and Learning (CTL), is 40 titles. In the lower grades, the numbers are similarly remarkable. Anne and her K–6 colleagues make time every day for students to curl up with books they love and engage in the single activity that consistently correlates with high levels of performance on standardized tests of reading ability: *frequent, voluminous, self-selected reading*. A child sitting in a quiet room with a good book isn't a flashy or, more significantly, marketable teaching method. It just happens to be the only way anyone ever grew up to become a reader.

And that is the goal: for every child to become a skilled, passionate, habitual, critical reader—as novelist Robertson Davies put it, to learn how to make of reading "a personal art."

Just as important, along the way we hope they'll become smarter, happier, more just, and more compassionate people because of the diverse worlds they experience within those hundreds of thousands of lines of black print.

The CTL faculty knows that students need time to read, at school and at home, every day. We understand that when particular children love their particular books, reading is more likely to happen during the time that's set aside for it—that the only surefire way to induce a love of books is to invite students to choose their own. So teachers help children select enjoyable books, develop and refine literary criteria, and carve out identities for themselves as readers. We get that it's essential that every child we teach be able to say, "These are my favorite authors, genres, books, and characters this year, and this is why." Personal preference is the foundation for anyone who will make of reading a personal art.

> *Personal preference is the foundation for anyone who will make of reading a personal art.*

Starting in kindergarten and going straight through until the end of high school, free choice of books should be a child's right, not a privilege granted by a kind teacher. Our students have shown us that opportunities to consider and reconsider books make reading feel sensible and attractive to children right from the start—and that they will read more books than we ever dreamed possible and more challenging books than we ever dreamed of assigning.

We've learned, too, that students need access to a generous assortment of inviting titles. Instead of investing in an expensive core reading program, our school makes individual books the budget priority. No child ever grew up to become a skilled, habitual, critical, passionate reader via a fat textbook.

And we've learned that we need to read a lot of the books we hope students will, so we can make genuine, knowledgeable recommendations, offer help as readers need it, and teach children one at a time in the daily, quiet conversations of reading workshop.

A fourth-grade reader lost in Raina Telgemeier's graphic novel *Smile*

Reading Is Comprehension

Finally, CTL reading teachers have learned, that the only delivery system for comprehension is *reading*. When reading is meaningful, understanding can't be separated from decoding. Comprehension isn't a set of sub-skills or strategies that children need to be taught. When kids are reading stories that are interesting to them and written near their independent reading levels, comprehension—the making of meaning—is direct, and they understand.

Human beings are wired to understand. As reading theorist Frank Smith puts it, "Children know how to comprehend, provided they are in a situation that has the possibility of making sense to them" (1997). Reading workshop is our best approximation of an instructional context that makes sense. A child sits in a quiet room with a beloved, accessible book in the company of classmates who are also reading and loving books and a teacher who knows about literature, reading, and his or her students, as readers and as individuals.

This is not a dream world; it's the way we've been creating readers since 1990. Because CTL is a nonprofit demonstration school—a place other teachers visit to learn about effective methods—we handpick a student body that represents a diverse range of socioeconomic backgrounds and ability levels. I raise money 12 months a year so we can set the tuition rate as low as possible and also provide generous tuition assistance. Our goal is to attract a mix of students in whom visiting teachers can recognize their own.

And they do, because CTL students are regular kids. They suffer ADHD, depression, and identified learning disabilities, including nonverbal learning disorders, visual-processing difficulties, and dyslexia. Some come from homes with packed bookshelves; some own only a handful of books. Maine is a rural state and a poor one. Less than half of the jobs here pay a livable wage, and our students' parents work hard as farmers, carpenters, daycare providers, soldiers, fishermen, cooks, gardeners, and housecleaners, as well as physicians, teachers, and small-business owners. So how and what our students read can't be explained away as an anomaly. This is not a privileged population of students. *This is what is possible for all children as readers.*

The Power of Pleasure

Which leads to the obvious question. If educators can agree that a goal of schooling is for children to become skilled, passionate, habitual, critical readers, why does so much of what goes on in the name of reading instruction *prevent* such reading from happening? The sheer waste of time, day in and year out, is mind-numbing as U.S. schools fall prey to standards and aligned curricula that have no basis in research, along with ambiguous and frustrating standardized assessments of reading, not to mention textbook-

A first grader encounters *The Very Hungry Caterpillar*

company promises that are questionable at best and, at worst, stunt children's growth as readers. Every day smart, well-meaning teachers are pressured to erect roadblocks between their students and the pleasures of the personal art. And there it is, the *P* word.

Reading workshop gives children pleasure, with minimal strings attached. This can drive middle-class Americans crazy (Newkirk, 1991). One legacy of our Puritan heritage and Protestant work ethic seems to be an unhealthy skepticism about any pedagogy that doesn't involve drill, self-discipline, and learning how to tolerate boredom and postpone gratification. But pleasure isn't immoral. Pleasure includes the enjoyment we find in artistry and beauty, in empathy and understanding, in thinking and learning and teaching.

America needs to get over it. When teachers of reading conceive of ourselves as literate grown-ups whose job it is to invite children to enter, again and again, just about the most pleasurable experience human existence has to offer, students will embrace books, enjoy reading, and become good at it. This is a noble endeavor. This is more than enough for society to ask of teachers or for us to ask of ourselves. To quote Robertson Davies again, the goal of the personal artist is "to read for pleasure, but not for idleness; for pastime but not to kill time; to seek, and find, delight and enlargement of life in books" (1959). This sounds to me like language for a job description: *Wanted: a teacher who can help children seek, and find, delight and enlargement of life in books.*

INSIDE THE READING ZONE

The Personal Art

scholastic.com/
RZresources

A fifth grader inhales *Mad Dogs* by Robert Muchamore

But open the door to many high school English classes or elementary school classrooms during reading time, in search of the authentic pleasures of the reading life, and what you're likely to find is a teacher talking and students taking notes, a teacher asking questions and students trying to guess the correct responses, or students filling in blanks, choosing the best answer, doing seatwork in groups, or prepping for the next round of standardized tests—everything, in short, but reading a book.

The more things change, the more they stay the same. When I was growing up in the 1950s and '60s, there were no actual books in any of my classrooms. Instead, we took turns reading aloud from basals in ability-based groups, where I got frequent raps on my knuckles with a teacher's ruler for looking ahead in the "story."

Later I graduated to the deadliest instructional approach ever devised by humans. The SRA reading program was a big box packed with color-coded cards, each of which featured a selection about a topic of no interest to any child, ever, followed by multiple-choice questions, followed by a teacher's corrections of the answers, followed by the next card prescribed by the student's results. This early version of "scientific, personalized" learning still makes me shudder—almost as much as its current iteration, scientific, personalized learning on a computer screen, which also claims to be individualized and competency-based but, like the SRA reading kit, thwarts authentic

> *Reading workshop gives children pleasure, with minimal strings attached.*

learning by omitting such essential conditions as motivation, engagement, collaboration with peers, and apprenticeship to a knowledgeable, trusted adult.

As a child, when I got home from school, I found no books there, either, apart from the World Book Encyclopedia, which my mother ordered and paid for a volume at a time when she could afford to. She worked as a waitress, my father was a mail carrier, and there wasn't money or time for books, or a family tradition of reading them. My saving grace was a neighborhood friend whose mother clerked at a drugstore and got a steep discount on the comic books her daughter asked for. I spent a lot of time at their house inhaling the adventures of Archie and Jughead, Little Lulu, and Milly the Model.

Then, when I was 10, my raggedy throat and aching joints were diagnosed as rheumatic fever, and I was sent to bed for six months to lie still and eat penicillin. When I began to grow crazy with boredom, my mother ventured into the local library in search of books she thought I might like. Through her efforts I met Beezus and Ramona, Henry and Ribsy, the March sisters, and the heroes of the Landmark biography series. I escaped my bed in the company of Clara Barton, Sam Adams, Lotta Crabtree, Jenny Lind, and Francis Marion, the Swamp Fox, and I vicariously experienced their perseverance and courage.

The day my mother delivered Frances Hodgson Burnett's *The Secret Garden* to my bedside, I wrinkled my nose at the musty cover and relegated it to the bottom of the pile. When, out of desperation, I finally cracked it open, it was just the right book at just the right time. I was Colin the invalid; I was Mary the obstinate; I was captivated and consoled. I read *The Secret Garden* four times that winter.

All that quiet time reading stories chosen for me by an adult who loved me changed me forever. Suddenly I had all these narratives inside me, all these people, and all this knowledge, not to mention a passion for books and the ability to read fast and with feeling. Graham Greene wrote, "There is always one moment in childhood when a door opens and lets the future in" (1940). This was my moment.

Now that I had the habit, I continued to read, but not the books I was assigned by teachers. Instead, I listened to class discussions, consulted Cliff Notes, and bluffed my way through *My Antonia* and *A Tale of Two Cities,* while at home I enjoyed an underground curriculum of my own devising—all of Orwell's novels (even *Keep the Aspidistra Flying*), Fitzgerald (but not *Gatsby*), James Michener, Ian Fleming, and that literary masterpiece *Rosemary's Baby*, which my girlfriends and I debated in furious whispers in the back of English class. As a high school student I enjoyed my social life. I didn't consider college; that wasn't a family tradition, either.

At the end of senior year, I learned that my scores on the New York State Regents Exam, combined with my parents' income, qualified me for free tuition to any state university. My mother, a Depression baby, said, "It's free. Why not give it a try?" So I enrolled at a local commuter college where they took all comers. And I loved it.

College was nothing like high school. Suddenly I had autonomy—I could read the course descriptions, or check out the titles in the college bookstore that were assigned by the different professors, and then pursue my own interests as a reader. I engaged full-throttle and eventually declared a major in English.

At the end of four years I had a Bachelor of Arts degree but no idea what to do with it. So I stuck around for an extra semester and did a stint of student teaching, calculating that education was a reliable fallback if nothing better turned up. The first time I took over a class, I knew I was home. I couldn't believe people got paid for spending their days talking with kids about books and poems and plays. More than 40 years later, I still can't believe it; my relationships with student readers—and writers—and my influence on their literacy have given me so much satisfaction.

Turning Mike Around: The Right Book at the Right Time

I lucked into my literary life. Schoolchildren shouldn't have to be lucky to discover that book reading is just about the best thing about being alive on the planet. Today the teachers of CTL do for our students what my mother did for me: search for books that will intrigue and entertain them, one child at a time. Nothing equals the power of the right book at the right time. Whether or not they have books in their homes, all students benefit when their teachers take care of them as readers—when we cultivate many and varied secret gardens so kids can discover *what reading is good for*, now and in their literate lives to come.

Take Mike. He moved to Maine from California and entered CTL as an eighth grader. On the reading survey our middle school students complete on the first day (p. 35), he wrote that sports was his favorite subject and comics his favorite genre to read. He couldn't name any book he'd like to read someday, identified no strengths as a reader, and wrote that his sole goal was "Staying with the book. Sometimes I doze off." He said he hadn't read a single book over the previous 12 months. He summed up his feelings about himself as a reader in one word: "Bad." At home that night, when I read his survey, I was so discouraged that I woke up the dog with my groans.

The next morning I asked him, "You read *zero* books last year? How can that be?" He explained he'd been given one big textbook in English class. The teacher assigned them to read a selection and answer the questions at the end. If the assignment was homework, he copied someone else's or didn't bother to do it, and if it was classwork, he "fake read." He explained, "Usually I played with a computer game that I hid behind the book while I fake read it." When I reviewed his school records, I found failing grades, standardized test results that placed him at the 15th percentile in reading, and a diagnosis of attention deficit hyperactivity disorder.

> *I am convinced that the lure of stories is a reading teacher's superhero power.*

Mike did not have a lot going for him as a reader. But what I had going for Mike as his new teacher was an unbeatable combination: a schedule with daily chunks of time for independent reading and a classroom library packed with great stories for all kinds of readers. I am convinced that the lure of stories is a reading teacher's superhero power.

In each day's reading workshop, students or I introduced books from my library— told a bit of the plot and problem and ended on a cliffhanger as an invitation to other readers. With Mike in mind, on the second day of school I booktalked three sports novels. He practically ripped one of them out of my hands, he was so eager to find out what happened next. It was the right book at the right time.

Mike finished Carl Deuker's *High Heat*, about a crisis in the life of a high school baseball player, in a week. Technically it was beyond his reading ability, but my introduction, a compelling plot and main character, his curiosity, and baseball enticed him into a fictional world and held him. When I circulated among the readers in his class to confer with them about their books, he could tell me what was happening and what he thought so far, and then he waved me away. He was *comprehending*. He was happy. That was all I needed to know.

Then he was on the lookout for the next book on his Someday List, a page of booktalked titles he had jotted down because they sounded intriguing. Mike's chosen genres included realistic fiction written for young adults (S. E. Hinton's *The Outsiders*, *The Absolutely True Diary of a Part-Time Indian* by Sherman Alexie, *Monster* by Walter Dean Myers, and *Son of the Mob* by Gordon Korman), fantasy (Orson Scott Card), journalism (*Friday Night Lights* by H. G. Bissinger and *Bringing Down the House* by Ben Mezrich), memoirs (*The Glass Castle* by Jeanette Walls was a favorite book), and horror (*The Reapers Are the Angels* by Alden Bell and Stephen King's *The Shining*).

Apart from reading workshop, the year my colleagues and I spent with Mike was a rough one. On days he didn't take his meds, he couldn't stay in his chair or keep his hands off the other kids. Even with a system of color-coded folders and binders, his papers were all over the school. He didn't keep accurate records of his work in any subject except reading; he didn't do homework in any subject except reading. His reading-writing handbook—a class notebook of ideas, plans, and information about literature and the craft and conventions of writing—was an unchronological mess of torn-out pages, caricatures of me, and notes about math, science, and history. And yet. And yet.

By June, Mike had finished 36 books. Without tests or quizzes, phonics instruction, strategy lessons, discussion questions, vocabulary lists, close-reading sessions, or digital platforms, he became an adept, motivated reader. He developed reading habits, critical abilities, preferences, and, for my money, one of the surest signs there is of full, rich literacy: he had plans for the books he wanted to read next.

Anyone's achievement, child or adult, is driven by interest. Until eighth grade, Mike had no reason to be interested in reading. But when he was offered vicarious adventures with characters he came to care for, he wanted to practice reading. Through voluminous practice, he became literate in the most authentic, productive sense of the word. He became a reader of books. And he became a better person— more knowledgeable about life, more curious and compassionate, attuned to a range of human experience, and a full-fledged member of a community of adolescent boys who defied the odds and talked about, traded, and liked books.

Students at our school assess their own progress as learners. In June, when I asked Mike's class to describe their breakthroughs as readers that year, he wrote:

> I never really read before. I'm picking out good books now. I'm enjoying reading. I'm noticing the way authors use details, create a theme, and make a movie in the reader's mind. I know when it's right to go through the whole text or just skim it. I notice when authors slow down the story so they can highlight the important stuff. I can put myself into the lives of the characters. I can tell when I'm bored, because I made a bad book choice, and find another book. I've learned what kind of books I like. I have three favorite authors: Walter Dean Myers, Gordon Korman, and Ned Vizzini. I love teenage dialogue, humor, strong characters, and strong themes. As long as I can choose good books, I will always like reading. That is my biggest breakthrough of all.

Instructional fads come, and they go. But human needs and desires remain constant. Every student—every Mike—whom we teach deserves the pleasure and meaning that literate adults find in the pages of books we love. Nurturing that love is the rightful work of reading teachers everywhere. It's not just a nice thing to do— it's the essential thing to ensure that our students become the skilled, passionate, habitual, critical readers we dream of.

Notice What Reading Workshop Is Not Doing

An American poet who consistently captures the admiration of seventh and eighth grade boys is William Stafford. My students often named his sly "Notice What This Poem Is Not Doing" as a favorite. Consider for a moment the nonsense that passes for reading instruction in too many of our schools by noticing what teaching reading in a workshop is *not* doing.

First, it's not telling kids they aren't smart or trustworthy enough to choose books and determine which ones are good and right for them. Virginia Woolf observed, "Literature is no one's private ground, literature is common ground; let us trespass freely and fearlessly and find our own way for ourselves" (1947). Reading workshop takes down the Keep Off the Grass signs. It invites young readers to explore and enjoy the lushest of landscapes, and, through booktalks, conferences, and conversations, it points the way to worthwhile, scenic routes.

Also notice how reading workshop doesn't impede the journey or exact a toll. There are no quizzes, notes, book reports, five-paragraph essays, reading logs, double-entry journals, or discussion questions between the last page of one good book and the first page of the next. Teachers who help and trust students to act as readers assess their growth in ways that match what readers do: we talk with them, listen to them, and show them what they need to know or do next.

Notice that there are no prizes or rewards for all this reading. The principal doesn't dye her hair green or host an ice cream party when the student body reads a million words. In reading workshop, the delights are intrinsic, always: *Today I got to experience a whole world with characters I loved; inside me I traveled, wondered, worried, laughed, cried, raged, triumphed.* There is no research evidence to suggest that rewards related to reading itself—say, a gift certificate to a bookstore—have any long-term benefit, but there are multiple studies that suggest just the opposite (see McQuillan, 1997; Marinak, 2003). In fact, for children who already like to read, studies of motivation show that when rewarded for an activity they enjoyed to begin with, kids are less likely to participate in it in the future, once the incentive is removed (Kassin and Lepper, 1984). In reading workshop, the vicarious adventures taken and the passions aroused by stories and characters, along with the development of a reading habit, are the prize.

> *Literature is no one's private ground, literature is common ground; let us trespass freely and fearlessly and find our own way for ourselves.*
> — *Virginia Woolf*

Notice how reading as a personal art doesn't contort or clutter the landscape with "reading activities." There isn't a find-the-root-word exercise, multimedia website, art project, prop or costume, bulletin board display, or extension assignment in sight. But there are rituals and systems—read-alouds, conversations, time, silence, comfort, simple reading records, booktalks, book reviews, and a classroom library that gets bigger and better every year, because the teacher understands that enthusiasm for reading and volume of reading are the keys, and everything else is a frill, boondoggle, interruption, or hurdle.

Notice how reading workshop teachers don't give kids misinformation about reading or bad advice. They encourage children to skim, skip, and look ahead. They view abandoning a book the reader isn't enjoying as a smart move, not a character defect. They *get* rereading and recognize that the desire to reenter a beloved book isn't cheating; it's a benchmark of someone who is becoming a personal artist. Nor do they confuse study skills with the aesthetic act of living inside a story, or insist that young fiction readers engage in such developmentally inappropriate activities as interrupting their reading to try to make connections. No one tells children they have to record and look up unfamiliar vocabulary. No one judges a child's fluency based on his or her proficiency at reading aloud cold, or limits book choices to a lexile level.

Making Reading Easy

While Anne and I recognize that this view flies in the face of both the metacognitive comprehension strategy movement and the Common Core State Standards, we maintain that one aim of reading instruction is to reduce frustration and distraction and *make reading easy*. We begin by understanding that for children, most of the act of reading stories lies below the level of consciousness and belongs there, as they are swept along in an indescribable stream of images and impressions. Reading workshop teachers forgo methods that interrupt the flow. And we acknowledge the guilt many of us grew up with—and can still feel—that there's a proper, rigorous way to read and somehow we're not doing it right, so we can help students navigate books with pleasure and confidence.

Also notice how reading workshop doesn't privilege informational texts over literature in response to the CCSS call for an ultimate balance of 70% nonfiction to 30% fiction in a child's school experience as reader. Workshop teachers understand that narrative rules. Mark Turner, a cognitive psychologist, positions story as "the fundamental instrument of thought. Rational capacities depend on it. It is our chief means of looking into the future, of predicting, of planning, of explaining" (1996). Whether factual or fictional, unless a text is a phone book, an actuarial table, some other kind of statistical display, or just plain poorly written, it tells a story: it moves a reader through time, as Thomas Newkirk argues brilliantly in *Minds Made for Stories: How We Really Read and Write Informational and Persuasive Texts* (2014). Newkirk posits that the CCSS suffer from a category problem by splitting texts into narrative, informational, and argumentative writing. Narrative—*causality*—is the frame that underlies every kind of good writing.

So reading workshop teachers fill the bookcases in their classrooms with many kinds of good writing because they know that students will learn—about the world and about the kinds of people they wish to become—from all of it: journalism, memoirs, autobiographies and biographies, science writing, satire, drama, poetry, *and* novels, as many as we can find and afford.

Finally, notice how reading workshop is not Sustained Silent Reading, not a study hall where we watch the clock with one eye as everyone Drops Everything and Reads. Teachers in a workshop are teaching readers for a lifetime. This means we check in with students about their books and progress. We prowl bookstores, professional journals, and websites for new titles and introduce them, along with worthy old favorites, to our classes. We teach about authors and genres, read aloud, talk with kids about their reading rituals and plans, and inform them about literary elements and terms. We discuss how to go beyond the four corners of a text and unpack a work of literature, how poems work, what efficient readers do—and don't do—when they come across an unfamiliar word, how punctuation gives voice to reading, when to speed up or slow down, which books won this year's awards, how to keep useful reading records, what a sequel is, what readers can glean from a copyright page, how to identify the narrative voice and tone of a literary work and why it matters, how the various purposes of reading affect a reader's stance and pace, how to recognize a genre novel or page-turner, how to determine if a book is too hard, too easy, or just right, how to ask for support when it's too hard, and why the only way to become a strong, fluent reader is to read often and a lot.

Reading makes readers. Frequent, voluminous, happy experiences with books—preferably in a room that's filled with good ones and in the company of a teacher who knows how to invite and sustain a love of stories—is the way to teach and learn reading for a lifetime.

> " Narrative—causality—is the frame that underlies every kind of good writing.

Reading workshop is one of the simplest and hardest things a teacher can do. It's also the most worthwhile. Students leave CTL as sophisticated, well-above-grade-level readers. They also leave just plain *smarter*, about such a diversity of words, ideas, events, artifacts, people, places, and times that they take our breath away. Books bring the whole world to a tiny school in rural Maine. When the children grow up and leave the school, they recognize the wide world they encounter out there because it is already lodged in the "chambers of their imaginations" (Spufford, 2002).

The Liberty to Read

High on a wall of her classroom hangs a quotation from Dylan Thomas that Anne has copied out in her careful printing: "My proper education consisted of the liberty to read whatever I cared to. I read indiscriminately and all the time, with my eyes hanging out ..." (1952). When Anne gazes out from her rocking chair over a sea of adolescents reading with their eyes hanging out, she recognizes education at its proper best. The room is still and silent because it has to be. Readers' minds are living other lives, learning to pose the questions that are worth asking, and filling up with the knowledge of the world.

CHAPTER TWO

Reading in the Zone

A third grader oblivious to the world and lost in the zone

Some students enter our school as kindergartners and begin to choose, read, and love books as five-year-olds. About half join us along the way, a few, like Mike, as late as eighth grade. Every September, when students come together to form the new seventh- and eighth-grade class, they represent a spectrum of middle school readers—different tastes, attitudes, abilities, and prior experiences. But by November, their common denominator as readers is that each of them easily and regularly gets lost in a book and enters the zone.

Jed, a seventh grader, coined the phrase. It's his interpretation of a condition Thomas Newkirk characterized as "the reading state" (2000). Newkirk wrote about his concern for the kids who don't like to read because they've never experienced the intense involvement, the "heightened form of pleasure" that kids who love books find themselves in all the time.

Defining the Zone

I gave students copies of Newkirk's article, curious about their take on it. It seemed to me that an inability or lack of desire to enter the reading state wasn't an issue for the boys and girls at our school. By Thanksgiving of any year, teachers of grades 1–8 can practically snap our fingers like hypnotists at the start of reading workshop, and every student is *there*. But why?

So I asked the seventh and eighth graders to think about three questions: Do you understand what Newkirk means by "the reading state"? If so, what's it like for you? And, if so, what conditions have teachers at our school established that make it possible for you to enter a state of engagement as a reader and stay there?

First, yes, every student, including those with reading difficulties, recognized what Newkirk meant by "the reading state." When Jed said it was more of a zone than a state, the phrase stuck. Individuals' answers to the second question defined the zone: the place readers go when they leave the classroom behind and live vicariously in stories.

Three-quarters of the kids compared the zone to a private, internal movie, *but better*. Nick, one of the stronger readers, wrote: "First of all, you see what's happening, in your head, like a movie screen. You care about the characters and think about what you would do at every point where they make a decision. You block out the sounds of the outside world. Eventually, it doesn't even feel like you're reading. You don't seem to be actually reading the words as much as it's just happening. And last, you don't want to stop reading."

Mark, a struggling reader, agreed: "When I'm in my reading zone, I feel like I'm a character in the book I'm reading. When I'm in my reading zone, it's almost like a TV show or a movie. I can see it really well. I can feel, taste, see, smell when I'm in my reading zone. Everything around you disappears and all you care about are the characters."

Students said that empathy plays a significant role in the zone. Many wrote about how they place themselves in relation to characters, something that happens unconsciously and automatically. Tyler noted, "It's hard to explain. It's like you're in the book, like right next to the

Jill Cotta, teacher of grades 3-4, booktalks *Poppy* by Avi

main character, but you're thinking his thoughts." Audrey wrote, "First, I have to be in a great book. Otherwise I don't want to enter it. But once I do, I don't always become the main character. Sometimes I become a best friend of the main character, someone who doesn't talk but just listens to his or her problems and joys. I feel as if the character needs me there, so I don't want to leave the novel." Forrest articulated a system for casting his mental movie: "Right away, literally, the second I start reading the first line, I begin formulating the 'movie' of the book. With girl characters, I am watching the 'movie,' but with boy characters, I am the star."

INSIDE THE READING ZONE

The Reading Zone
scholastic.com/
RZresources

Most students described a fugue-like state when absorbed in a book: "I forget where I am and who's around me and even who I am." "You don't notice that you're turning pages or going on to the next chapter." "You're not aware of the page number or what technique the author used or what the theme is." "Time goes by incredibly fast, but I'm not aware of it at all." "You get lost, but in a good way." For young readers, comprehension, stamina, and the absence of distractions have everything to do with getting lost in the zone.

The Top 10 Conditions That Sustain the Zone

Finally, each student described the classroom conditions that make this level of absorption possible. Forrest, a seventh grader who had been at our school for just six months, wrote that in order to enter the reading zone, he discovered he needed:

- encouragement from the teacher and advice.
- time to read at school.
- trillions of great books as backups.
- silence, absolute silence, to help be transported into "The World."
- booktalks to recommend great books.
- comfortable cushions and pillows.
- a healthy chunk of time to read at home every night.

I categorized all the kids' responses—what the members of the group perceived as essential if a language arts class is to be transformed into a reading zone. In the order in which they were most mentioned, these are the top school conditions my students said make engaged reading possible, not to mention likely.

> *For young readers, comprehension, stamina, and the absence of distractions have everything to do with getting lost in the zone.*

1. Booktalks and mini-lessons (cited by 88% of respondents)

2. A big, diverse classroom library with regular new additions (74%)

3. Quiet, daily, in-class time to read (73%)

4. Individuals' free choice of books, authors, and genres (56%)

5. Recommendations of books from friends and the teacher and a special bookshelf for kids' favorites (54%)

6. Comfort during in-class reading time (53%)

7. Students' letter-essays to the teacher and friends about their reading (53%)

8. Individuals' conversations with the teacher about their reading (31%)

9. Individuals' lists of the books they want to read someday (30%)

10. Homework reading of at least half an hour every night (30%)

Quiet and Comfort

A condition I felt special gratitude for was the kids' acknowledgment of a reader's need for quiet. After 30 years of teaching reading in a workshop, I still suffered twinges of guilt whenever I asked students to stop talking. *But they're talking about books! They're socializing about literature!* And they weren't reading. And they were distracting the readers around them, bumping them out of the reading zone. And if I didn't remind them about the silence rule, I was giving everyone else permission to stop reading and start talking, too.

So it's quiet during the workshop. But when the reading diet is rich, the reading environment extends on its own. Students who enter the zone find plenty of opportunities when they emerge from it to talk with friends about books they love, just as I do in my life as a reader, just as you do in yours.

If the sounds of speech during reading are a distraction, so is music, even classical compositions. For some children, any noise makes absorption difficult. This includes the noise a teacher makes. While my students read, I moved among them to chat about their books, and I whispered. Readers whispered in response; if they didn't, I said, "Please whisper." Every September I taught a lesson about quiet during reading workshop as an act of thoughtfulness in all the senses of the word. And the first week I asked the group, at the end of independent reading time, to talk about how hard or easy it was to enter the zone in a room filled with other people. Most kids said it took them two or three reading workshops each fall to feel comfortable reading in a group again, even a quiet, thoughtful one.

Fifth-grade readers get comfortable on whistle cushions

A seventh grader lounges on a beanbag as she begins a new book

Young readers find that psychological comfort is easier to achieve when they're physically comfortable; hence the vinyl-covered beanbags and whistle cushions that CTL students can sprawl on as they read. At a school where I'd previously taught, the principal was irked to no end by the sight of adolescent readers sprawling. It offended his sense of decorum. So I learned to spare him by covering the window in the classroom door with a sign: DO NOT DISTURB. READERS AT WORK. And even with their feet up and their heads down, they were.

Nightly Reading

I was surprised when almost a third of the kids mentioned nightly reading as a condition essential to their presence in the zone—it must have pained them to have to admit any benefit to homework. But given the constraints of middle school, there isn't enough time during class for kids to become skilled, passionate, habitual, critical readers, even with a block schedule like mine and Anne's. After a discussion of a poem, a mini-lesson, and independent writing time, her students get 20 to 25 minutes in the zone each day: not as generous as she would like, but enough time to engage and to understand why reading is one of the priority activities of her classroom and their lifetimes and should be carried on at home as well.

The baseline homework, the most important assignment any teacher can give, is reading. At CTL, we ask all students, K–8, to take their books home with them every afternoon, read or be read to for at least half an hour, and bring the books back the next morning. When Anne circulates among readers during the workshop, one of her whispered queries is, "What page are you on?" She records the title and page number on a status-of-the-class form she carries on a clipboard. With few exceptions, a student who isn't at least 20 pages beyond yesterday is in homework trouble.

Every student in grades 5–8 begins the year with a homework pass in each subject: one time when a teacher will excuse uncompleted work. After that, for each missing assignment, we mail home a form letter to parents that explains what wasn't done and asks for their help. After three letters, we schedule a meeting with the student and parents to discuss how we can work together to help the child come to school ready to participate in class activities.

When the missing schoolwork is the nightly half hour of reading, the focus of the conference is on *why*: Is there no obvious place at home for the child to read? No obvious time? Is the student forgetting to take home his or her book? Do the parents and child understand the importance of frequent, voluminous reading to his or her future as a student and a human being?

Kindergarten teacher Caroline Bond and students love a book together

We are not hoping that frequent, voluminous reading will happen. We are using everything we know about books and every system we can invent to make sure it does, starting with students' free choice of great stories and ending with homework letters and parent-student-teacher conferences if a child is having a hard time developing the reading habit and carrying the zone home.

The remaining conditions for engaged reading named by my former students are big topics that deserve ample time and space. In subsequent chapters we'll explore choice, conferences, the classroom library, booktalks, writing about reading, and the practical logistics of reading workshop.

In looking back at the big picture of what students said compels them to enter the reading zone and stay there, what strikes me most is how aware they are of what they need in order to act as engaged readers, and how little of what they name has anything to do with a method or a program. Reading teachers don't need new instructional techniques. The goal is straightforward: figure out how students can enjoy and sustain relationships with books and, as readers, with their teacher and one another.

Supporting the Zone: Three Kinds of Teacher Knowledge

When my seventh and eighth graders read Newkirk's article and considered what makes it possible to enter the reading zone, only one wrote something along the lines of "Having a teacher who loves to read books." To tell the truth, I was miffed. Here I was, demonstrating passionate literacy all over the place, and virtually nobody noticed. I asked them about it in class. "Why do you think just one of you cited a book-loving teacher as important? What am I here, the wallpaper?"

Jed said, "Well, yeah, you are kind of like wallpaper. We take it for granted that our teachers love books." When students grow up in a school where the faculty likes books, often noisily, it's a given that reading teachers are grown-ups who live for the personal art.

I grounded my teaching of reading in what I know as a practitioner of the personal art. I thought about what stories do for me in my life, and what they could do for my students. I hoped they'd want to apprentice themselves to me and trust that what I asked them to do mattered, made sense, and offered satisfaction. And I wanted them to take advantage of my experiences as a reader, just as I assimilate the knowledge of my teachers, past and present, who love the personal art.

Effective teaching of reading begins not with the right method, system, strategy, or program, but with the wallpaper: what teachers know of books, reading, and the kids. I think three kinds of teacher knowledge are at work when students immerse in the pleasures of the zone and grow as readers.

INSIDE THE READING ZONE

Professional Knowledge

scholastic.com/ RZresources

1. The teacher's experience as a reader: our encounters with books and the reading we do about books, authors, reading, and teaching reading.

If we're to invite kids inside the zone, we need to know the territory, not just children's and young adult literature, but also novels, memoirs, essays, journalism, and poetry written for adults, as well as writing *about* literature: reviews, critical essays, and journal and newspaper articles. And we need to read about the teaching and learning of reading. Louise Rosenblatt and Frank Smith are my foundation. I also depend upon Richard Allington, Marie Clay, Shelley Harwayne, Stephanie Harvey and Anne Goudvis, Stephen Krashen, and Thomas Newkirk. To those who protest they don't have time to read, Daniel Pennac says, "I've never had time to read. But no one ever kept me from finishing a novel I loved" (1992). Teachers need to grant ourselves the joy of good writing and grant our kids the knowledge we gain when we read their books, our books, *and* professional journals, websites, and books.

2. The teacher's knowledge of the needs and tastes of readers of this age—third graders, middle schoolers, high school sophomores, or whomever our students may be.

The teaching questions I brought to a grades 7–8 workshop were the same every year: Who are middle schoolers? What are their concerns, strengths, idiosyncrasies, and ambitions? Who's writing well for them? What books will help them grow up, make them think, laugh, cry, and gasp, knock them out? What journals and websites are reliable for reviews? Which bookstore collections are productive to browse? It's a big responsibility to build a classroom library and keep it up to date, diverse, and compelling. But without intriguing books close at hand, students won't—*can't*—enter the reading zone, let alone find a home there.

3. The teacher's knowledge of particular students—of each reader's interests, preferences, strengths, and challenges.

We need to forge relationships with kids around books: What is *this one* reading? Why? How? How do I help her move forward? How do I support him as he builds a reading identity so he can lay claim to his tastes, processes, and criteria and say, "These are my favorite books, the authors I love best, the genres I enjoy most, the poets whose poems resonate for me. These are my rituals—the times and places I read. This is how I read a novel, a poem, an article, a scientific report, a challenging book, an easy one. This is when I speed up or slow down. This is when I decide to abandon a book, this is when I stick with it, and this is when I can't put it down. This is how I choose books. And these are my plans—this is what I want to read next."

The three kinds of knowledge comprise a reading teacher's pedagogical money in the bank. We can never know everything about books, reading, and our students, but we can keep making deposits and become smarter—more purposeful, more generous in our invitations, more responsive to what each reader is trying to do, more aware of the ways and reasons that people read, and less likely to buy into the "evangelical promotion of" new and improved approaches to teaching reading that are "misguided at best and simply profit oriented at worst" (Allington, 2012).

> *Effective teaching of reading begins not with the right method, system, strategy, or program, but with… what teachers know of books, reading, and the kids.*

Welcome Students to the Zone

Our students appreciate the solitude of the reading zone, and the quiet. They know how to be happily alone with a book. But they also recognize that they need the experiences of other readers to keep themselves going. *This* is the rightful work of a reading class and a reading teacher. The ultimate delivery system for voluminous reading is a deliberate environment that invites, nurtures, and sustains immersion in stories and characters, that says every day of every school year, *Welcome to the zone.*

What About ebooks?

Ebooks have been a recent topic of discussion among Anne and her kids. When students who have access to electronic devices that store books try them out in the workshop, every one of them reverts to paper books. Why? The kids' answers are illuminating.

They say they miss the physicality of book reading—what Anne calls "the topography of an open book." Its two pages and eight corners help readers orient themselves and create a mental map of the journey, versus a single page of screen that's constantly changing. Plus they get essential tactile feedback by holding a book: the fingers of the right hand tell them how many pages remain for the author to resolve the plot. And they're able to flip back and forth with ease to clear up confusions. They have more control over a text—if it's their own copy, they can highlight it, dog-ear it, and write in the margins. They tell Anne and me that it's not possible to browse among ebook titles as they can with paper books. They complain about glitches that lose their places and the inconvenience of being tethered to a cord while an ebook is charging. Most significantly, they feel they remember more of what they read when the book is made of paper.

Two recent studies back up the last assertion. In one (Mangan, et al., 2013), tenth-grade students who read a paper text scored significantly better on a reading comprehension test than students who read the same materials digitally. In the second study (Mangan, et al., 2014), adult Kindle users were significantly worse than book readers in placing the plot events of a short mystery story in the correct order. Mangan and her teams make many of the same points as our kids do, plus one more: scrolling is such a consistent distraction that comprehension and retention both suffer.

For Anne and me, the biggest impact of ebooks that we've observed is social. Students find identity and camaraderie in the physicality of paper books, where the covers function like badges they wear to class. Without them, kids miss the book chat—the thrum of opinions, advice, questions, and enthusiasms—that's voiced every day in a community of book lovers. It's hard to reap the social benefits of reading if you're carrying around a grey screen.

CHAPTER THREE

Choice

A sixth-grade reader raves in a booktalk to his classmates about *The Wild Robot* by Peter Brown

Daniel Pennac perfectly titled his paean to reading (1992). He called it *Better Than Life*. The frontispiece of the book is Pennac's list of what skilled, passionate, habitual, critical readers know but that teachers and parents can forget, don't understand, or do appreciate for themselves but withhold from children. Our seventh and eighth graders read and debate it the first week of school.

Some of Pennac's ideas defend *how* a reader might read. His argument for reading out loud provokes the most discussion, because many student readers, both struggling and strong, have a hard time performing aloud without practice. To his "right not to finish," our kids have added "or to read just the ending." And they've proposed a number 11: "The right to free access to lots of good books."

The Reader's Bill of Rights

1. The right not to read something
2. The right to skip pages
3. The right not to finish
4. The right to reread
5. The right to read anything
6. The right to escapism
7. The right to read anywhere
8. The right to browse
9. The right to read out loud
10. The right to not defend your tastes

Daniel Pennac (1992)

Most of Pennac's ideas address *what* someone might read. Our kids voice the strongest support for the right to their own tastes as readers. And they appreciate Pennac's justification for free choice of books: "Our reasons for reading what we do are as eccentric as our reasons for living as we do."

In the classrooms at CTL, choice is a given. Kids choose what they read because children who choose books read more, read better, and are more likely to grow up to become adults who read books. Students who read only a steady diet of assigned titles don't get to answer, for themselves, the single most important question about book reading: why would anyone want to? As William Dean Howells put it, "The book which you read from a sense of duty, or because for any reason you must, does not commonly make friends with you" (1902).

We can no more pick *the* book that will invite a whole class to make friends with reading than we could decide whom our students should grow up and marry. It's that personal, that chemical, that idiosyncratic, and, yes, to us anyway, that important. For students of every ability and background, it's the simple, miraculous act of reading a good book that begins to turn them into readers, because even for the least experienced, most reluctant reader, it's the *one good book* that changes everything. The job of adults who care about reading is to move heaven and earth to find and put that book into a child's hands.

For Anne, the job begins on the first day of school, when she asks students to complete a survey about who they are as readers and what their own good books might be. The questions are formatted over two pages, so there's plenty of room for students to respond. The survey can easily be abridged and adapted for kids in the younger grades.

INSIDE THE READING ZONE

Choice in Reading and Writing

scholastic.com/ RZresources

> " *Kids choose what they read because children who choose books read more, read better, and are more likely to grow up to become adults who read books.* "

Reading Survey

1. If you had to guess…

   a. How many books would you say you owned? _____

   b. How many books would you say there are in your house? _____

   c. How many books would you say you read during the last school year, September–June? _____

   d. How many of *those* books did you choose for yourself? _____

   e. How many books would you say you've read since school let out in June? _____

   f. Do you think you read *a lot* of books, about *average*, or *less than average*, compared with other kids your age? _____

2. What are the three best books you read in the last year or two? _____

   _____

   _____

   _____

3. What are your favorite genres, or kinds, of books to read? _____

   _____

4. Who are your favorite authors these days? List as many as you'd like.

   _____

   _____

5. What are some of the ways you decide whether you'll read a particular book?

   _____

   _____

   _____

6. When and where do you like to read—what's your favorite place and time? _____

   _____

7. Have you ever liked a book so much that you reread it? _____ If so, what's the title?

   _____

8. In your ideal book, what would the main character be like? _____

_____

_____

9. What are the causes or issues—political, cultural, science-related—that you care about?

_____

_____

10. What do you do for fun after school or on weekends? _____

_____

_____

11. What else are you interested in? _____

12. What do you think are your three greatest strengths as a reader of books? _____

_____

_____

_____

13. What would you like to get better at as a book reader? Try to think of three goals.

_____

_____

_____

14. Do you know the title or author of the next book you'd like to read? _____

If *yes*, what is it? _____

15. Why do you read? _____

_____

_____

16. On a scale of 1–10, how do you rate book reading? _____

17. In general, how do you feel about yourself as a reader?

_____

_____

Anne reads the completed surveys and takes notes on a chart she makes for each class, which she carries with her during independent reading time on the class's workshop clipboard. Her notes capture the data from the answers to the first question as well as students' favorite titles, genres, and authors (if any); reading habits (again, if any); personal interests; the specificity and tone of their self-assessments; if they've ever reread a beloved book, which is a good sign; if they have plans as readers, an even better sign; and how they perceive reading, books, and themselves as readers. And then she gets to work, planning booktalks and trying to match the titles she knows with the readers she is getting to know.

The Importance of the Classroom Library

The work that's never done centers on the classroom library and finding and replacing enough good books so there are titles for everyone and no reader gets left out. To reach that goal, we need to have on hand *at least* 20 books per student. I know that budgets are tight everywhere, but in terms of getting bang for a buck, nothing matches the impact of classroom libraries. Multiple studies have documented that there are more books in the classrooms of high-achieving schools and more students who read frequently (Krashen, 2011). Richard Allington writes, "If I were working in a high-poverty school and had to choose between spending $15,000 or more each year on books for classrooms and libraries, or on one more (teaching assistant), I would opt for the books...Children from lower-income homes especially need rich and extensive collections of books in their school..." (2012).

When I was teaching, several times a month I visited a local bookstore with a reliable collection of young adult literature as well as inviting transitional titles—books by such writers as Margaret Atwood, Michael Chabon, Junot Diaz, Dave Eggers, Jonathan Safran Foer, Mark Haddon, Nick Hornby, Kazuo Ishiguro, Barbara Kingsolver, Yann Martel, Cormac McCarthy, Tim O'Brien, and David Sedaris—that give adolescents a taste of what comes next

Part of the kindergarten library, in the school's Primary Reading Room

for them as independent readers. In the bookstore, I grazed, picking up every title that looked possible, bearing in mind authors and imprints that were already popular, and thinking of individual students and what they liked.

I sat with the stack and skimmed the first pages or chapter of each title and felt lucky when I found three or four I could imagine putting into a reader's hands or booktalking with enthusiasm. Then, when I purchased them, I made sure I received the teacher discount. Again, since we're not investing in or replacing expensive anthologies, the entire reading budget at CTL is dedicated to individual titles.

I also read book reviews, as Anne does today. We appreciate the reviews in NCTE's *English Journal* and *Voices from the Middle*. The school subscribes to *Booklist*, which is published monthly and includes reviews of new titles for grades K–12, and the excellent

The grades 3–4 library in CTL's Reading Room

A first grader peruses a book from her group's collection in the school's Reading Room

An eighth grader signs out her next book from the grades 7–8 library in the school's Humanities Room

VOYA, published monthly and geared toward grades 7–12. We also keep a lookout for issues of *The New York Times Book Review* that include reviews of children's books, read the reviews on amazon.com and Goodreads, and, on the last Sunday of the month, log on to #titletalk.

We've learned, too, which awards and citations matter in selecting books for seventh and eighth graders. On the back cover and inside the front cover of a paperback written for a young adult audience, we look for:

- ALA (American Library Association) Alex Award Winner
- ALA Quick Pick for Reluctant Young Readers
- ALA Top Ten Best Book for Young Adults
- ALA Alex Award Winner
- ALA Quick Pick for Reluctant Young Readers
- Coretta Scott King Award
- *Kirkus Reviews* Editors' Choice
- Michael Printz Award for Excellence in Young Adult Literature
- National Book Award Winner or Finalist
- New York Public Library Books for the Teen Age
- Reference to a *starred* review in *Kirkus Reviews*, *Publishers Weekly*, *Booklist*, *The Horn Book*, or *School Library Journal*
- *School Library Journal* Best Book

> *You can't catch a cold or a love of books from someone who has neither.*
> — *Jim Trelease*

When I was teaching, I read a lot of young adult literature, and I did love it. Today, that's Anne's responsibility. During the school year her reading diet is about two-thirds young adult titles and one-third personal and professional reading. As a reading workshop teacher, she has to know the books that are written for her kids and, just as important, appreciate them. As Jim Trelease put it, "You can't catch a cold or a love of books from someone who has neither" (2013).

At the same time, a teacher of reading workshop in grade 4 and up can't read every single book. First of all, no one will have that much time and everyone already suffers enough teacher guilt about the perfect job we should be doing. Our advice is to read as many kids' titles as you can, as fast as you can. On a quiet weekend morning I could inhale at least one, often two.

But I also have to confess that I couldn't bring myself to read some of the books. These included science fiction, where Vonnegut is my limit, quest fantasies, and vampire sagas. Since I had students who loved—or would love—these genres, it was my responsibility to give them advice and direction.

So I learned to pay attention to the experts in my classroom—to ask them to teach me and their classmates about their genre specialties. And I handed off new titles to students I thought would appreciate the books and asked if they'd be willing to preview them and, if good, booktalk them to the group.

Booktalks

I wasn't surprised when students named booktalks as the top condition essential to their engagement as readers in a workshop. It's not enough to stock a classroom library with great books. We also need to use our voices to bring life to the tattered spines that line our shelves and make sure that kids inform other kids about titles that are too good to miss, so everyone is exposed to a diversity of genres and authors and has plans for what he or she wants to read next. This is essential to the health of a reading workshop.

When I was teaching, a class of students and I conducted 250–300 booktalks every year. This means that a kid or I sat in my rocking chair for a couple of minutes and told a bit of a story we loved: who the main character is, his problem or hers, the genre, maybe a theme of the book or what made us love it or how we read it, and, always, a numerical rating. Then the booktalker took questions and passed the book along to its next reader. The online resources for *The Reading Zone* (see scholastic.com/RZresources)

Ted DeMille, teacher of grades 1–2, introduces a new picture book

include videos of booktalks by two seventh graders: Hope on *These Shallow Graves* by Jennifer Donnelly and Griffin on *March* and *March, Book 2* by John Lewis and Andrew Aydin.

A booktalk is a combination of community service and sales pitch. It's not an oral report. It's never graded. Other than the book, there are no props or audiovisuals—no notes, either, unless a reader feels he or she needs them. Booktalks are short, direct, informal endorsements of titles that individual readers love and that haven't been booktalked yet that year. Again, the purpose is to introduce

Glenn Powers booktalks *Raymie Nightingale* by Kate DiCamillo to grades 5–6

as many great reads as possible. When a booktalked title had been named by other students in the class as a favorite, I asked at the end, "Would you raise your hand if you loved it, too? Is there anything you want to add?"

When Anne appreciated a young adult novel by John Corey Whaley, she introduced it to her class in a booktalk:

> This is *Noggin* by John Corey Whaley. I loved it. I rated it a 10.
>
> Sixteen-year-old Travis is the main character. He's waged a long battle with leukemia, which he's on the verge of losing. His girlfriend, Cate, his best friend, Kyle, and his family are all heartbroken. So his desperate parents enroll him in a medical program that cryogenically freezes him, in hope that someday advances in science will find a cure.
>
> Cut to five years later, when a kind of "cure" has been found. It's now possible to attach Travis's healthy head to a donor's body. (Trust me. Whaley makes this work.) He's alive, but everything is different. Cate, Kyle, and everyone he knows are five years older, while he's still 16. Cate's engaged, and Kyle's still hiding the secret he confessed to Travis on his deathbed. Travis has to go back to school with new peers whom he remembers as being little kids. And something is off with his parents.

INSIDE THE READING ZONE

Booktalks by Hope and Griffin

scholastic.com/ RZresources

Aside from its sci-fi premise, *Noggin* is totally convincing as realistic fiction because Travis is so funny and relatable as he navigates this impossible situation. He has to reconsider his whole identity along with everyone he knows—or thought he knew.

I like how Whaley adds elements that careful readers will love to notice, like how the last few words of each chapter become the title of the next. He's a good writer *and* a good storyteller. His *Where Things Come Back* and the latest, *Highly Illogical Behavior,* are also 10s and novels that kids and I have loved. John Corey Whaley is a name to know.

Questions? Does everyone know what a *noggin* is? Is anyone interested in taking it?

With one exception, I learned not to promote a book that I didn't rate as a *9* or *10* out of 10; I asked my students to uphold the same standard. After a lukewarm review—even a *7* was the kiss of death—that book sat exactly where it was put down for the rest of the school year. I broke the endorsement rule with new titles I hadn't read yet by explaining what about the book had led me to buy it, reading aloud its back or jacket flap copy, and asking who'd like to try it first.

To sign up to give a booktalk, a student slipped an index card with his or her name on it inside the book and put the book on a designated shelf, at the end of the row. At the start of a reading workshop, I plucked the first two or three titles from the beginning of the row and called up those booktalkers, so the order was always first come, first served.

When a contest broke out after a booktalk over a title that sounded especially attractive, the student or I did the time-honored, fair thing and asked anyone who wanted the book to raise a hand and guess the number the booktalker had in mind. The closest guess got the book, and the others recorded the title on their individual lists of books they planned to read someday.

I tended to booktalk several titles together, often in relationship to one another. In addition to *new titles I love* and *new titles I haven't read yet*, there was *a worthy genre for your consideration, a worthy author, a worthy series, beloved classics, YA oldies but goodies, a collection by topic, a collection by theme, top picks for the weekend*, which ensured everyone had enough good books to carry him or her through until Monday, and *good fast reads*, for struggling readers who were looking for intense action and main characters whose motivations were unambiguous.

Books-We-Love Displays

When the *Kids and Family Reading Report* (2007) surveyed American readers between the ages of five and 17, they discovered that almost a third of middle school students and almost half of 15- to 17-year-olds read only *two to three times a month*. The number one reason kids cited for not reading more? They couldn't find books they wanted to read.

Classroom libraries of great, age-appropriate titles, along with heartfelt introductions, make books they *will* want to read visible to kids, available, and attractive. And a personal record-keeping system like a Someday List makes it easy for readers to recall intriguing titles (Figure 3.1). It's hard to make plans when you don't know what your options are. By briefing kids about the great stories still waiting for them, booktalks help students select, reject, develop criteria, and look ahead.

I also developed a nonverbal way for students to recommend books to one another. Each class at our school has its own Books-We-Love case or stand where children showcase their favorites as a service to their peers. Students—not teachers—select the titles on display there. Sometimes a student booktalks a beloved title before adding it to the collection; sometimes a reader just puts the beloved book here, instead of reshelving it. The Books-We-Love display case was the hearth of my classroom,

FIGURE 3.1 The first page of an eighth-grade boy's Someday List

Glenn and a student search the grades 5–6 collection for a book on the boy's Someday List

A fifth grader checks out the Books-We-Love display for his class

now Anne's. I'm certain that if you tracked down our former students in a decade and asked them what they remember about reading workshop, many would reply, "Books We Love." Kids choose at least half the books they read from this collection. It is the trustworthy, peer-tested, dynamic centerpiece of the reading workshop.

Three times a year, the K–8 boys and girls at our school contribute to master lists, organized by grade level and gender, of inviting, accessible titles. The lists contain the books students name in response to this question: *What books do you love so much you think they might convince a(n) ___ grade girl/boy who's a lot like you—except that she/he doesn't read much—that book reading is great?* The answers are available to our students and their parents over the summer, as well as other teachers and the general public, on the "Kids Recommend" page of our website, c-t-l.org.

Students update the list often because the fields of children's and young adult literature change so quickly. While a handful of titles maintain their popularity over years—S. E. Hinton's *The Outsiders* (1968), the novel that created young adult literature, continues to speak to kids—most drop off and are replaced. I'll never again publish between the covers of a book a list of must-have titles for a classroom library because it will be out of date before the ink is dry.

> " *I'm certain that if you tracked down our former students in a decade and asked them what they remember about reading workshop, many would reply, "Books We Love." "*

Students' Books-We-Love Displays

Grades 1–2

Grades 3–4

Grades 5–6

Grades 7–8

Complex Texts

Middle school teachers who download "Kids Recommend" from the CTL website will find titles that aren't typical middle school reads—*A Clockwork Orange*, *The Amazing Adventures of Kavalier and Clay*, *The Sun Also Rises*, *Brave New World*, *One Flew Over the Cuckoo's Nest*, *Catch-22*, *Emma*, *Fahrenheit 451*, *Rebecca*, *Bel Canto*, *Slaughterhouse-Five*.

One of the many good things that happens in a K–8 school where reading workshop is a way of life is the growth in students' abilities and interests as readers. Many seventh and eighth graders choose, understand, and like books that I only read as an adult. I'm thinking of Abe, who read and appreciated Machiavelli's *The Prince* and Bulgakov's *The Master and Margarita*, which he found among his mother's books from her college years. Then there was Ridgely and *Moby-Dick*, Wallace and *Crime and Punishment*, Tess and *The Scarlet Letter*, Nicco and *The Great Gatsby*, Amelia and *The English Patient*, and Carolyn and all things Austen.

Lexile levels have nothing to do with choices like these. Experience does. A non-reader confronted with an assignment of *Huck Finn* or *Pride and Prejudice* doesn't stand a chance. But a student who enjoys years of access to good books and generous time to read them can become astonishingly literary in terms of well-above-grade-level ability, curiosity, self-confidence, sophistication, and stamina. Honestly, it can be hard to keep up with them. At Abe's urging, I read Bulgakov for the first time.

Middle school teachers who download "Kids Recommend" will also encounter titles they'll recognize as having been challenged in other communities. In almost every case, the challenged book was assigned to a class by the teacher. In 30 years of teaching reading in a workshop in both private and public schools, I can count on the fingers of one hand the occasions when parents raised concerns to me about a book a student was reading. A reason I experienced so few censorship problems is that I wasn't distributing a class set of, say, *The Catcher in the Rye*, and requiring every student to read it. Instead I shelved a copy or two in the classroom library for students who were interested and ready. And, in the end, I bowed to individual parents' wishes for their individual children.

> " *One of the many good things that happens in a K–8 school where reading workshop is a way of life is the growth in students' abilities and interests as readers.* "

Honoring Parents' Values

Will's dad called me one September evening because Will, a seventh grader from a devout family, had brought home a novel that featured swearing and some sexual activity. His father said he was offended by the language and thought Will was too young and inexperienced for the book's plot and themes. I replied, "I absolutely respect your values, not to mention your sense of what's best for Will. Please let him know your objections to the book, and first thing tomorrow I'll help him look for a more appropriate choice. And thanks for calling me—I want you and Will's mom to be supportive of his reading and comfortable with his books. I've got tons of other great titles I can put in his hands."

On a Monday morning of a different autumn, Zack's mother approached me in the school parking lot to complain that the Robert Cormier novel her son had read over the weekend had shaken him up. "He was upset all day yesterday," she said. "The harsh things that happened to the main character really troubled him. Zack can't handle books like this. He's more of a fantasy reader, I think." Again I said, "Thanks for telling me. You know, I'm just learning who Zack is, as a person and a reader. Some of the authors who write contemporary realism for young adults can be pretty bleak in their outlooks. I'll steer Zack away from this kind of book. I want his reading to satisfy him, not disturb him."

The insights and concerns of a student's parents mattered to me. So when a mother or father spoke to me about a book choice, I responded in the context of the particular child. Censorship is less likely to become an issue when each child chooses his or her books *and* when the teacher has read most of the books and knows what's in them. If put to the test, I could defend every title in my classroom library as to its worth and its appropriateness for other students.

Book Quality and Abandonment

This means that in addition to purchasing books, I returned them. When I read a young adult novel or the start of a series and couldn't find anything of value in it, I asked for the school's money back. I tried hard not to buy junk—there is always more than enough of it available to my students in pop culture—and I found myself steering clear of young adult authors who it seemed to me were edgy or morbid for the sake of being edgy or morbid. I didn't purchase many adult bestsellers, either, because they're often *so bad*. On occasion I borrowed a popular page-turner from the local library or downloaded a chapter, read some of it aloud in a mini-lesson, and asked kids what they noticed. For students who had been reading literary young adult fiction, these books are a shock: "How can this be a bestseller? Who could read that and think it's good writing?"

But at the same time as students recognized that Dan Brown and Michael Crichton don't reliably craft lucid prose or develop plausible characters that readers can care about, they also said, "The writing did bother me, but not as much as the plot grabbed me. I was turning the pages like crazy just to see what happened next." There are insights to be gained even from a page-turner—understanding the distinction is a huge one. The insights come in the context of continuous conversations about what makes a book worth a reader's time.

There are too many good books out there waiting for readers to waste precious time with books we don't enjoy. Students need more than permission to abandon books that don't satisfy them. They need encouragement from a teacher, and even the occasional cease and desist order.

A student who hasn't found that one good book yet will sit for days with a title that bores him because he doesn't know how the reading zone feels. Teachers need to be confident enough to take books *out* of readers' hands when they're not loving them, and then help them consult their Someday Lists, or pull three or four titles from the classroom library or Books We Love as new possibilities. And we need to ask students to think and talk about their criteria for book abandonment: how many pages will you give a book to become compelling before you pull the plug? The most important *should* in reading workshop is that students should read for the joy of reading. Once they have the reading habit, the books themselves will form their tastes.

Delight and Responsibility

Children's author Philip Pullman wrote, "True education flowers at the point when delight falls in love with responsibility. If you love something, you want to look after it" (2005). One way we show children we love them is by looking after them as readers. Only when we invite them to discover the books that delight them will they cherish literature and their own literacy.

> " *The most important* should *in reading workshop is that students should read for the joy of reading. Once they have the reading habit, the books themselves will form their tastes.* "

Make Reading Easy

In the CTL faculty handbook, the section on reading instruction opens with a quotation from Frank Smith: "Children learn to read only by reading. Therefore, the only way to facilitate their learning to read is to make reading easy for them" (1983).

I put it there to brush away, right from the start, the cobwebs—and outright spiderwebs—of the long history of frustrating, cumbersome methods for teaching reading. Smith reminds us that when it comes to reading, the teacher's job is to understand it, notice what needs to be taught, teach it, and *ease the way* for students to become skilled, passionate, habitual, critical readers.

The box of book-borrow cards for the readers in grades 3–4

This is pretty much the opposite of what I was taught in my undergraduate methods courses. There I learned how to teach assigned novels, a chapter at a time, with discussions, tests, and even essays at the ends of chapters. The emphasis was dual: make it hard—*rigorous* was the preferred term even then—and make students prove they had read the books, got what they were supposed to get, and understood there are right books to read, right ways to read them, and that it should hurt.

Learning to read and read well are already hard enough. It takes years of practice to make knowledge of English texts automatic, transparent, and fluid. When children practice reading in a context that's kind—with books they love, teachers who understand reading, and systems devised to make a difficult thing doable—they're more inclined to practice, remember, make sense of, get better at, and enjoy reading.

To make reading easy for students, the bottom-line requirement is an inviting classroom library, organized so it's simple for children to find books and return them. The Dewey Decimal System doesn't have a place here. Instead, teachers need to put books together in ways that help young readers find what they're looking for, even if they don't know what it is yet.

Thirty-five years ago, when I began to learn about young adult literature, my classroom library was a crude arrangement of three categories of books, fiction, nonfiction, and poetry. Today Anne shelves over 1,500 titles alphabetically by authors' last name in bookcases labeled in useful, inviting categories: memoirs and biographies, journalism, humor, fantasy, science fiction, dystopian sci-fi, paranormal affairs, thrillers, horror and supernatural, sports fiction, historical fiction, war and antiwar, free-verse narratives, graphic narratives, adult and transitional fiction, poetry anthologies by theme, poetry collections, essay collections, short story anthologies and collections, classics, Shakespeare, other drama, and, the largest grouping, contemporary realistic fiction. In addition, her students maintain their Books-We-Love collection, where 60 or so titles are displayed with covers facing front so they're inviting and accessible.

Over years of reading workshop, I lost a lot of books from my classroom library. While one part of me delighted that students were loving books so much they were borrowing them forever, another part fumed at the cost—both the price I paid to purchase a book and the lack of availability of a title to other readers. I went back and forth between elaborate checkout systems, which ate up my time, and freedom from systems, which ate up my books.

What worked, finally, was the simplest method of all. Teachers in grades 3–8 staple together five index cards for each child and label this packet with the child's name. We put the packets in an unlidded box, one box per class, along with a pencil or two. When a reader borrows a book, he finds his packet of cards in his class's box and writes down the new title. When a reader returns a book, she brings her card packet *and* the book—the ocular proof, as we like to say—to the teacher, who draws a line through the title and writes his or her initials next to it. Then the reader reshelves the book or adds it to the Books-We-Love collection. I most often initialed titles back into the classroom library as I circulated among students during independent reading time. Today, instead of a quarter or more of the volumes disappearing forever, only a handful go missing each year.

Taking Books Home

To make book borrowing, reading at home, and book returning easier for younger readers, CTL provides a means of conveyance. The school hires a parent with a sewing machine to construct overnight bookbags for students in grades K–4. We use bright, sturdy fabric remnants to create 16-by-12½-by-3-inch bags with double handles made from 1-by-26-inch straps of webbing. This gift from the school is a child's to keep for the year and another demonstration of the value we place on books and reading. The teachers help each K–4 student be certain there's a book or three in the bag at the end of reading workshop to go home that afternoon and return via the bookbag in the morning. In June, we collect the overnight bookbags; wash, repair, and replace them as necessary; and then put them back to work in September.

Older students wouldn't be caught dead carrying bright, sturdy, fabric bookbags. They carry their books back and forth between school and home in backpacks. But their teachers, too, make sure that every student *has* a book to pack up every day at the end of reading workshop.

And to make home reading easier for all our students, we never assign busywork in connection with the pleasures of book reading. There are no home-reading slips, book reports, sticky notes, logs, notebooks, double-entry journals, or other documentation to check up on, test, eat the time of, or kill the joy of readers. We trust that the books are great. We trust that the kids will love them. We understand that any reader lost in the zone dreads the prospect of busywork when he or she closes a book, and we recognize that it *serves no purpose.* Because the teachers meet with students during reading workshop, they ascertain daily whether everyone is liking and understanding his or her book.

> *Because the teachers meet with students during reading workshop, they ascertain daily whether everyone is liking and understanding his or her book.*

Matching Books to Readers:
Holidays, Challenges, and Just Rights

The approach we use to determine whether a title is a good match with a young reader's abilities was developed by Leslie Funkhauser, a second-grade teacher in New Hampshire (Hansen, 1987). When students are responsible for selecting the books they read, they need to be able to differentiate between titles within their reach that they can read with accuracy and understanding, and those they aren't ready to tackle independently. Research shows that anything less than 98 percent accuracy slows a reader's growth and "anything below 90 percent accuracy doesn't improve reading ability at all" (Allington, 2012; Ehri, Dreyer, Flugman, and Gross, 2007). So we define three levels of book difficulty, teach kids how to put the definitions to work, and use the terms in conversations about books.

For each student, a given title is either a Holiday or easy read; a Challenge, which will require some assistance; or a Just Right, that is, a book that's a bit of a stretch in terms of the child's current level of skill. An easy test for a Just Right in grades K–5 is Jeanette Veatch's "rule of thumb" (1968). A reader turns to a page in the middle of the book he or she is considering, reads it silently, and puts down a finger at each unfamiliar word. If the child hits five words—uses all four fingers and a thumb— that's an indication the title is too difficult to be read with accuracy and without frustration.

Students are not forbidden to read Challenge books, because sometimes a child's interest in a story, subject, or author is the prevailing factor. With these books, we teach kids that they'll probably need to seek support from an adult or another student, as in a dyad or reading buddy approach (Eldredge, 1995); recognize that the book will take a longer time to finish; and/or read an annotated version. For example, when my students wanted to tackle

Jill conducts a mini-lesson for grades 3–4 that reviews the three levels of books

Shakespeare independently, I bought annotated copies of three of the plays from the No Fear Shakespeare series, and they happily ate *Hamlet, Henry V,* and *Much Ado about Nothing* after I booktalked them.

However, if a child consistently chooses Challenge books, the teacher would intervene because of the impact on accuracy, understanding, and volume. The rule of thumb isn't immutable. But as a guideline it keeps the emphasis where it belongs, on continuous, high-success practice and the satisfaction of experiencing and finishing many books. In a fall newsletter to parents about reading (included in Chapter 10), we teach parents about Holidays, Just Rights, and Challenges, so they can, at home, continue to help children do what they're trying to do as readers.

CTL teachers appreciate the accessibility of three simple-to-determine levels—instead of a whole alphabet or onerous lexiles—because it labels books, not children. All readers have our own Holidays, Just Rights, and Challenges. The categories help students consider where they stand in relation to a particular book at a particular moment in their reading lives without undermining their confidence by labeling them or narrowing their experience to selections predetermined to be written at the right "level."

> *We tell students what we know, what we notice they know and don't know yet, and how they can better do and understand what they're trying to do and understand.*

Teaching Beginning Readers

The teachers of CTL do *teach reading.* We tell students what we know, what we notice *they* know and don't know yet, and how they can better do and understand what they're trying to do and understand. In mini-lessons to the whole group, taught before individuals settle into independent reading, we provide information, conduct demonstrations, and lead discussions that help children make sense of all kinds of books.

At the primary level, this means that Caroline Bond, at kindergarten, and first- and second-grade instructor Ted DeMille teach lessons about the strategies that beginning readers use to identify unfamiliar words in the books they're reading. They show the children how to look at the beginning letters of a word; use what they've learned about letter sounds, including from their own writing, to determine and see if sounding out will help; look at an illustration for clues; listen for a repeating pattern or a rhyming pattern; look for a little word they do know inside the bigger word they don't; skip the unfamiliar word, read the rest of the sentence, and then come back and try it again; use a placeholder word and just keep going; try to recall if they've seen the word before somewhere else; and ask for help.

Kindergarten word work: a shared reading of a poem

Caroline and Ted also teach procedural lessons about what reading workshop should look, sound, and feel like. They introduce high-frequency words and teach children how to read one another's names. They discuss when it pays to reread and when it's better just to keep going; how readers pause and breathe at a period; why and how to keep track of finished books; how to take a bookwalk through a picture book; how to preview front- and back-cover blurbs and chapter titles to determine where a chapter book is headed; how to mine the table of contents, index, glossary, and diagrams in nonfiction texts; and the elements of stories—plot, character, setting, problem, climax, and resolution. They also engage their students, via read-alouds and discussions, in studies of authors and illustrators whose books offer generous invitations to beginning readers: Jan Brett, Eric Carle, Donald Crew, Tomie dePaola, Lois Ehlert, Mem Fox, Gail Gibbons, Kevin Henkes, Shirley Hughes, Leo Lionni, Arnold Lobel, Bill Martin, Jr., Robert McCloskey, Else Holmelund Minarek, Jerry Pallotta, Patricia Polacco, Maurice Sendak, William Steig, Mo Willems. Caroline and Ted read aloud hundreds of fiction and nonfiction storybooks every year, and they help their students read, recite, and sing hundreds of poems, songs, chants, recipes, and messages they've printed on chart paper.

In addition, Caroline draws on the remarkable work of her predecessor as CTL's teacher of kindergarten, Helene Coffin, and Helene's book *Every Child a Reader: Month-by-Month Lessons to Teach Beginning Reading* (2009), by incorporating poetry in her reading workshop. During her tenure Helene collected a multitude of lively examples of contemporary verse written for children. She copied the small, fresh stories and images onto oak tag charts, to become the heart of the kindergarteners' word work. Using Helene's lessons, Caroline introduces one or two new poems every week, with the results a double blessing. The children learn to decode with exuberance, and all of them achieve fluency and independence by year's end. The rhythms, patterns, repetitions and cadences, imagery, diction, and brevity of great poetry for kids, along with the meaningful experiences and observations the poems relate, engage kindergarteners and invite voices filled with interest, understanding, and expression.

On the following page you'll find a sample schedule from Helene Coffin that describes reading opportunities throughout the day in a kindergarten classroom.

Reading Throughout the Day in Kindergarten

8:45–9:30

CIRCLE TIME During this block, I implement certain literacy routines each day: the "Special Helper's" name exercise (naming the letters and sounds in a classmate's name), the recitation of the letters and sounds on an alphabet chart, the reading of sight word cards, the reading and discussion of poems, a word study, and a picture book read-aloud.

9:30–10:15

MATH To begin our calendar routine, students review the letters and sounds in the name of the current month, and I often read picture books aloud to introduce or reinforce math concepts.

10:35–11:15

READING WORKSHOP At the beginning of reading workshop, students participate in a shared reading of the class message. Afterwards, I present a mini-lesson, for example, an author study, cloze activity, or "Making Words" activity. The final segment of reading workshop is independent reading. Students select their "just-right" books to take home for their 30-minute reading homework, and then they read or browse other selections while I listen to individual children read aloud, assess their progress, advise them about their "just-right" book selections, and teach or reinforce different reading strategies.

11:15–12:00

WRITING WORKSHOP Students learn about writing conventions and craft by drafting simple memoirs, poetry, and letters. They write spelling approximations by segmenting sounds and recording the corresponding letters for the sounds they hear. Students also have portable word walls they use to spell high-frequency words correctly. I often read aloud picture books to demonstrate a specific craft element.

12:05–12:25

LUNCH Every day at 12:15, an eighth grader reads aloud a story while the kindergartners finish their lunches.

1:00–1:30

REST TIME READ-ALOUD/READING BUDDIES During rest time, kindergartners listen to chapter books, which help to strengthen their listening comprehension and love of story. On Fridays, they meet with their fourth-grade reading buddies to read poems aloud from their poetry notebooks, practice the sight words on their individual word rings, practice decoding strategies as their buddies provide assistance, and listen to stories read by the fourth graders.

2:00–2:20

CHOICE TIME During this block, kindergartners often choose to read books, act out stories, or perform puppet shows.

READING HOMEWORK Each student from kindergarten through eighth grade reads (or is read to) for 30 minutes every night.

Adapted from Coffin (2009).

Instruction at the primary level should result in joy, purpose, skill, personal preferences, and a sense of community. This represents a parallel universe to the nonsense lessons that dominate most core reading programs for beginning readers, which confuse looking busy with reading and deny young children the pleasures of the zone.

Teaching Older Readers

At the other end of the K–8 spectrum, Anne teaches lessons that make it easier for individuals to enter the zone and get their feet under them as opinionated, versatile, critical readers who have goals and plans. Many of the lessons are booktalks. Each involves kids in a discussion of good books and good things that smart, versatile readers know and do.

Anne and her students review the expectations and rules for reading workshop. They discuss how and why to develop criteria for choosing books and abandoning them; the usefulness of keeping a personal reading record and a list of Someday books; and how the act of looking for and naming favorites—books, authors, genres, poems, poets—eases the way to becoming both a satisfied reader *and* one who is in charge of his or her literary life. Anne asks kids to think about the different stances readers take in relation to different kinds of texts (Rosenblatt, 1978; 1994) and to consider criteria for pace—when do readers decide to speed up, slow down, skip, skim, or look ahead? They discuss why and when readers want to reread books and poems, and they name the genres they're reading (the most recent genre summary Anne's students collaborated on appears in Chapter 10).

Anne teaches her students about the books, styles, lives, and perspectives of authors and poets who write well for middle school readers. She shows them how poetry works in terms of form, sound patterns, diction, compression, and its use of figurative language and how to read and unpack a poem. She illustrates such elements of literary fiction as character development, pace, plausibility, narrative voice, climax, tone, conflict, and theme, and she accounts for the differences among a vignette, short story, novella, and novel. Appendix C, *What We Talk About When We Talk About Stories*, is a handy, focused reference Anne created for herself and shares here for other teachers' use. It's a kind of grammar for talking about narratives. In September she asks students to set aside half a dozen pages in their writing-reading handbooks for the literary lexicon they'll create together each year (Atwell, 2015). Then, when a concept comes up in a booktalk or mini-lesson, she teaches the relevant term and kids record it and its definition.

> *Instruction at the primary level should result in joy, purpose, skill, personal preferences, and a sense of community.*

After a student has booktalked *To Kill a Mockingbird*, Anne defines a term for inclusion in the story lexicon

As readers and writers Anne and her students also tease out the features of effective essays, memoirs, parodies, book reviews, profiles, and short fiction. She relates relevant details about how book publishing works—royalties, printings, copyright dates, jacket blurbs, and the hardbound-to-paperback route—and introduces resources from the worlds of publishing and scholarship that are worthwhile for middle-school readers to know about, including *The New York Times Book Review*, Amazon.com, *Benét's Reader's Encyclopedia* (Murphy, ed., 1996), *Literary Terms: A Dictionary* (Beckson and Ganz, 1980), and Ron Padgett's *The Teachers and Writers Handbook of Poetic Forms* (1987).

Preventing Distractions

Reading mini-lessons that Anne and her colleagues *don't* conduct include instruction about comprehension strategies kids should employ and text features they should look for as they read stories. Practices like these hurt comprehension because they distract and interrupt children—tell young readers to stop being engaged and, instead, to make connections, find significances, notice how a book was written, even take notes. In addition, these behaviors counteract the way children's brains are wired. Because, like everything else about the human animal, what happens when we read changes over time.

Neurologists posit that cross-referencing and critical scrutiny during the act of reading are more functions of the mature brain and less that of developing ones (Fair, et al., 2009). When children read, the affected regions of their brains interact mostly with neighboring regions. However, comprehension-wise, theirs are just as efficient at processing information as the brains of adults. (In fact, in the 2009 study, seven-year-olds showed they're just as smart as grown-ups when given access to the same information and asked to perform tasks with it.)

As we mature, our brains form more diffuse circuits and experience longer-range interactions. This creates new networks and, for readers, new distractions—a development that makes it less likely for adults to achieve the deep immersion that child readers enjoy. One neurologist suggests that because the mature brain is so prone to making associations and comparisons during reading, "an adult reading experience may be a 'dip' compared with the child's 'soak'" as, unbidden, diffuse networks interact and, without our intending it, relate a text to people, things, events, and texts we've previously experienced (Prose, 2016).

INSIDE THE READING ZONE

Ease

scholastic.com/ RZresources

I can remember when I was 10 years old and still had the ability to be soaked—to immerse 100% in a good story. Now, it's rare, and I cherish it when a book comes along that lets me reexperience that intensity of thought and feeling—it happened most recently with Louise Erdrich's novel *LaRose*, which I lived inside of and didn't want to leave when the story ended. Mostly, though, I dip in and out of the reading zone, since the circuits of my brain can't help but light up with memories, with inferences, with observations about the writing. Of all the ways the CTL faculty has determined not to deny children their childhoods, our insistence on preserving the reading zone is near the top of the list.

So we appreciate Francis Spufford's beautiful memoir about reading, *The Child That Books Built* (2002), because it almost captures the experience of a child soaking in the zone. I say *almost* because this is how it must be. For kids the processes of story reading are so subtle, so fantastic, so quicksilver and simultaneous, that we can't account for them, measure them, test them, or teach them. We can only give them great books and time to get lost in them, and then be grateful when a reader who writes as well as Spufford goes spelunking in the zone.

In the meantime a child is sitting reading. Between the black lines of print and the eye, a channel is opening up [through] which information is pouring; more and faster than in any phone call, or any microcoded burst of data fired across the net, either, if you consider that these signals are not a sequence of numbers, not variations on a limited set of digital possibilities, but item after item of news from the analogue world of perception, each infinitely inflectable in tone and intent. The Prince sighs as his sick horse refuses to take sugar from his hand. Oatmeal sky over dank heather. It is a truth universally acknowledged that a man in possession of a fortune must be in want of a wife. Engage the star drive! Yet the receiving mind files away impression after impression. (Sometimes, to be sure, only in a mental container marked DON'T GET IT.) This heterogeneous traffic leaves no outward trace. You cannot tell what is going on by looking at it: the child just sits there, with her book or his. It cannot be overheard, makes no incomprehensible chittering like the sound of a modem working on a telephone line. The subtlest microphone lowered into the line of transmission will detect nothing, retrieve nothing, from that incalculable flow of images.

The goal of Anne and her colleagues as planners of reading lessons is to provide students with information that's useful and true. In combination with useful time—all the hours at school and home devoted to reading stories and inhabiting the zone—most of our students ease their way into becoming skilled, passionate, habitual, critical readers. But even with smart, sensible teaching, some children will struggle. We give these students slightly different vehicles for entering the zone.

When Readers Struggle

Some of our struggling readers lack experience with books. They come to CTL with normal intelligence but a background of nonsense instruction in reading. The standardized reading test results in their cumulative records place them anywhere between one and three years below grade level.

> *Every year I felt the September challenge and the midwinter satisfaction of having nudged my inexperienced readers into the zone through stories that compelled them to believe in books, practice reading, and perceive themselves as readers.*

More than anything that a school might provide them, these readers need surefire stories written near—or not impossibly above—their independent reading levels, and time to read them. They need *pleasure*. Teachers dedicate ourselves to the search for the first book that will deliver it; most often it's a novel with a strong plot and larger-than-life characters. Frequent, sustained, voluminous reading will bring these readers up to grade level. Every year I felt the September challenge and the midwinter satisfaction of having nudged my inexperienced readers into the zone through stories that compelled them to believe in books, practice reading, and perceive themselves as readers.

Some struggling readers are boys and girls who struggle in general, with intelligence below average norms but no evidence of learning disabilities. These kids, too, deserve to read at the top of their ability range *and* enter the zone easily and joyfully. So we add to the classroom library, booktalk, and recommend titles for readers who still have difficulty interpreting subtleties of motivation or theme, who don't yet appreciate ambiguity, irony, or figurative language but still want and deserve the zone.

For these two groups of middle school readers, the inexperienced and the challenged, imprints such as Orca Soundings, Saddleback Publishing, and Lorimer Books, and authors such as Kwame Alexander, Meg Cabot, Sarah Dessen, Sharon Draper, Gayle Forman, Mel Glenn, Jenny Han, Geoff Herbach, S. E. Hinton, Anthony Horowitz, Gordon Korman, Emmy Laybourne, Walter Dean Myers, Louis Sachar, Sonya Sones, and Rachel Vail succeed in creating strong characters and plots that transport them into the reading zone.

Other struggling readers cope with identified learning disabilities that interfere with their ability to process text. Their intelligence ranges from average to far above, but their performance as readers, affected by dyslexia or other processing difficulties, does not. Because of neurological differences, they can't access all the cuing systems that other readers rely on. But they can develop and retain sight vocabularies that, eventually, allow them to read with fluency, understanding, and pleasure. Here, a key is linking auditory and visual input, especially during the primary and intermediate years.

One method to try with readers in grades K–2 is dyad or buddy reading (Eldredge, 1995), in which a struggling reader is paired with a fluent reader—a classmate, an older student, or an adult—who provides scaffolding for a unison reading. The two sit side by side and share one book. The better reader sets the pace, reads aloud with fluency and expression, and, with "one SMOOTH finger," touches each word as he or she says it, while the assisted reader looks at the words and tries to say them right along with the lead reader.

The buddies typically read together for 10 minutes at a time. The books are children's literature self-selected from a crate of titles that are one or two grade levels above that of the struggling reader, since research (Morgan, et al., 2000) shows that materials that represent minor challenges lead to the most growth in word recognition, comprehension, and fluency during dyad reading.

Ten years ago, a parent of a CTL third grader diagnosed with dyslexia contacted the National Library Service for the Blind and Physically Handicapped. Through their talking books program, NLS loans thousands of audiobooks on CDs that are recorded to play at slower-than-standard speed. They also provide headphones and specially adapted CD players, all available at no cost, sent and returned by postage-free mail, through a network of cooperating regional libraries.

Talking books are a godsend for students who qualify for the program. Jill Cotta, who teaches our third and fourth graders, believes that the speed control is key: children are able to slow down the reading rate of a selection until they can follow the words with their eyes. She also notes that the adult voices on the NLS audiobooks read at one pace, without special accents or pitches customized for different characters, and there are no sound effects or background music to distract readers from the sound and sight of one word after another in the books they've chosen. Talking books help young students'connect auditory and visual input, enter the zone, and, over time, develop sight vocabularies that begin to compensate for reading disabilities.

To be eligible for the program, a sighted child must be certified by his or her physician as having a physically or visually based disability severe enough that it makes it difficult to read books. Students with nonorganic reading problems—short attention spans, emotional issues, deprived backgrounds, different first languages—don't qualify. The child's parents apply for talking books on his or her behalf, their physician signs the application form, and, if approved, only that student may use the audiobooks and special CD or mp3 player. If a child is a legitimate candidate for talking books, the process is simple and quick. The NLS publishes online catalogs of available audiobooks on their website at www.loc.gov/nls/. Jill helps students select titles from the classroom library; then she or a parent orders the accompanying audiobooks, usually three at a time. Most often, the talking books arrive in the next day's mail or can be downloaded right away.

In the intermediate grades, our struggling readers experience tremendous success with regular audiobooks. Glenn Powers, a teacher of grades five and six, helps his students with reading disabilities choose books they're interested in from the listings on OverDrive, an app that gives teachers free access through public libraries to books-on-CD. CTL also has an Audible.com account with an ever-growing collection of titles picked out by Glenn and his students. He perceives steady benefits in high-interest Challenge titles read at a conversational pace with inflection, natural phrasing, and appropriate emphasis. The student wears earbuds as he or she listens and reads along, seeing each word as it is said, "chunking" the text in response to the prosody of speech, and improving both word recognition and comprehension.

Becoming a Reader: Samuel

I remember the final pupil evaluation team meeting I attended on behalf of Samuel, an eighth grader who had been diagnosed with dyslexia at age eight. The purpose of the PET was to determine whether he should continue to be classified as a special education student in high school. His parents and I argued it wasn't necessary, because in the past two years Samuel had read 38 books on his own. All the hours he'd spent reading along with someone else's voice in the primary and intermediate grades, and then entering the zone independently in middle school via characters and stories he loved, had given him a sight vocabulary that would choke a horse. But the special-ed tester from the school district that Samuel's family lived in insisted he was still disabled and, as evidence, reported the results of his latest screening. He still couldn't sound out a list of made-up morphemes.

A sixth-grade student reads and listens to a book at the same time

If this is how someone chooses to define reading—the pronunciation of isolated nonsense syllables—then Samuel would never become a reader. But bring on great *books*, and he could read virtually any title he picked up. His continuous experiences with prosody and the built-in redundancies of English syntax and semantics, his acquired memory of the shapes and sizes of thousands of words, and his interest in stories enabled him to vault over his dyslexia and read. Sam entered high school as a regular student, achieved the honor roll every trimester, and excelled in college.

At CTL we haven't made a single scientific breakthrough in reading instruction. Instead, we try to notice what individual children can and can't do in the context of reading real books, and then look for ways to ease the process. And we make sure that students who need the *most* sense and satisfaction—those who struggle as readers—get it.

James Baldwin said about books, "You think your pain and your heartbreak are unprecedented in the history of the world, but then you read. It was books that taught me that the things that tormented me most were the very things that connected me with all the people who were alive, or who had ever been alive" (1963). Only a reading teacher

Instead, we try to notice what individual children can and can't do in the context of reading real books, and then look for ways to ease the process. And we make sure that students who need the most sense and satisfaction— those who struggle as readers—get it.

who opens wide the door to the zone can ensure that *all* students experience the mutuality of the human race. Only in books will children experience the people, ideas, events, and feelings that make existence comprehensible. Strong readers *and* struggling readers want to know the joys and sorrows of other lives, the common dreams that unite us, and the satisfactions of great stories. Teachers help by making reading *as easy as possible* for all our students all the time.

I think most reading teachers know this. But we get sidetracked by trends in methods or misled into believing there's a magic bullet, or we're told by administrators to adopt approaches that waste students' time and kill their interest in reading.

An Influence for a Lifetime

This is why tenure was invented. Contrary to propaganda, tenure exists not to protect the job security of bad teachers but to safeguard the decisions of smart teachers about what matters and how best to help children learn it. A tenured teacher in a district that mandates nonsense can call it that. He or she can do what good teachers have always done: close your door, observe your kids, collect data, and make professional decisions about what's best for the students you teach. When it comes to reading, a teacher pressured to use a mandated program can shortcut it wherever and however possible, invite frequent, voluminous, happy encounters with books whenever possible, and create a haven for readers that will influence those kids for a lifetime.

CHAPTER FIVE

Checking In

Trying to maintain a balance in the workshop between worthwhile discussions with the whole group and individual conversations with readers was a constant, healthy tension in my teaching. Some of what I know about reading and literature proved to be inspiring, thought-provoking, or useful to the class, but often what a student needed most wasn't a discussion or a demonstration but a quick chat with me about how things were going.

I learned to watch the clock and limit the length of mini-lessons and booktalks, so readers could read and I could talk with and teach them one at a time when I circulated during independent reading time.

Jill checks a third grader's progress in his book

I bumped readers out of the zone by asking for just enough reflection that I could monitor their progress and satisfaction and glean their observations and opinions.

INSIDE THE READING ZONE

Checking In

scholastic.com/
RZresources

The original title of this chapter was "Conferences," but as I was writing it, I paused to speak at a regional meeting of teachers, where there was a fair amount of anxiety during a Q&A about how to confer with independent readers. Teachers said they struggled with what to say when every student was reading a different book. They were flummoxed about how to discuss books they hadn't read yet. Most significantly, they worried about not meeting frequently enough with individual readers. One teacher told me it was all she could do to confer with each of her students once a week.

> *...the primary purpose (of checking in) is making sure that everyone is okay—in the reading zone and happy to be there.*

Perhaps because it seems to suggest a sustained session about a topic of great import, the word *conference* can misdirect or even intimidate teachers. *Checking in* is a more accurate, less freighted way to describe my and Anne's meetings with readers, where our primary purpose is making sure that everyone is okay—in the reading zone and happy to be there. Our check-ins with kids aren't oral exams, for them or for us, about the books. One-to-ones cannot wait from one week to the next, especially for students new to reading workshop. A weeklong gap is long enough to hurt a struggling reader's motivation and momentum for months.

So Anne checks in with each student every day by asking the basics: "What are you reading?" or "How is it?" or "What do you think so far?" or "Are you (still) happy?" and, always, "What page are you on?" She keeps track of the book titles and page numbers on a status-of-the-class chart (Figure 5.1). And that's it for teacher record-keeping in our reading workshops at CTL once students have learned how to read.

Anne and her colleagues in grades 1–6 capture what's essential about a student's day-to-day progress as a reader: he has a book, or not; he likes it, or doesn't; he is, or isn't, reading at home at night; he's finishing books and finding new ones, or else that's not happening yet and the teacher needs to step in right away.

> *When a student isn't reading in the zone, Anne follows up by finding out why.*

When a student isn't reading in the zone, Anne follows up by finding out *why.* She might ask, "If you were going to rate this book right now, what number would you give it?" Anything lower than a 7 is a sign that a reader should abandon the book and try another. Sometimes she's more direct: "Will you consider abandoning this one? Because if you're not hooked by now, I can't see that it's going to happen. There are too many great stories waiting for you to waste precious reading time on a book you don't love. C'mon, let's look at your Someday List together."

Nolan	Nicco	Kaleb	Joe	Emma	Katie	Lucas	Sydney	Jolie
Monster (106)	Great Gatsby (1)	Noggin (92)	Painting the Black (57)	The Red Pencil (110)	Since You've Been Gone (3)	Life of Pi (31)	The Glass Castle (76)	And Then There Were None (220)
" (191)	" (34)	" (126)	" (102)	" (226)	(453)	" (76)	" (107)	" (272)
" (243)	" (67)	" (195)	" (168)	" (309)	I Am Malala (12)	" (34)	" (167)	" (306)
To Kill a Mockingbird (1)	" (88)	" (287)	" (210)	The Help (48)	(86)	" (184)	" (202)	The Book Thief (10)
" (78)	" (102)	" (340)	The Martian (20)	" (165)	(179)	" (221)	(261)	" (105)
" (164)	" (130)	Into Thin Air (25)	" (104)	" (243)	(284)	" (289)	Unexpected Everything (1)	" (216)
" (243)	" (168 BT)	" (81)	" (179)	" (337)	(342)	" (327)	" (49)	" (324)
(301)	Unbroken (3)	" (154)	" (293)	" (471)	Stop Pretending (10)	Storm of Swords (41)	" (151)	" (417)
(370)	" (151)	" (203)	abs.	(520) (BT)	" (101)	" (92)	" (246)	" (526)
Peak (54)	" (230)	" (290)	" (423)	To All the Boys.. (10)	The Scarlet Letter (1)	" (210)	" (307)	Vengeance Road (7)
" (113)	" (346)	No Summit out of Sight (1)	The Road (1)	" (92)	" (37)	" (279)	(BT) (388)	" (48)
" (212)	" (423)	" (89)	The 5th Wave (AB)	" (176)	" (86)	" (334)	" (441)	" (105)
The Edge (13)	Infinite Sea (27)	" (177)	" (109)	" (269)	" (110)	abs.	" (500)	" (189)
" (91)	" (98)	" (281)	" (217)	" (345)	" (139)	" (571)	Poisonwood Bible (1)	" (248)
" (156)	" (189)	(340) (BT)	" (334)	P.S. I Still Love You (1)	Life as We Knew It (12)	" (746)	" (41)	(BT) (303)
" (208)	" (261)	All-American Boys (8)	" (452)	" (56)	" (49)	Feast for Crows (1)	" (105)	Are Animals as Smart... (1)
The Glass Castle (10)	The Things They Carried (1)	" (67)	Naked (1)	" (104)	" (117)	" (197)	" (181)	" (53)
" (64)	" (42)	" (105)	" (25)	" (179)	" (188)	" (242)	" (243)	" (108)

FIGURE 5.1 A page of Anne's status-of-the-class chart for reading workshop

Process questions like these are part of Anne's repertoire, as are questions about the craft of writing. Some of the concepts and terms that inform her conversations have roots in writing workshop, for example, in mini-lessons about narrative voice, plot structure, diction, dialogue, time shifts, pace, and character development. Appendix B: What We Talk About When We Talk About Stories: A Lexicon is a collection of terms she uses and introduces to kids when talking with them about their books. Some check-in questions help students articulate their literary criteria. Others ask kids to venture an assessment of an author's choices, or rescue readers who need a strategy to untangle themselves. Some queries help them make plans. One monitors homework reading. A question Anne does not ask until after a reader has finished a book is, "What do you think the theme is?" Most young readers aren't able to take that particular critical stance—naming the ideas that emerge from a story—until they've had a whole, coherent experience of it. Some old readers, too, me included.

Checking In With Readers: Some Questions We Ask

ALWAYS:

• What page are you on?

MOSTLY:

• What do you think so far?

• How is it?

• What's happening now?

• Are you happy?

• Are you still happy?

AND ALSO:

• Any surprises so far?

• How did you feel/what did you think when you got to the part where…?

MAIN CHARACTER QUERIES:

• Who's the main character in this one? What's he or she like?

• What's his problem?

• What's the conflict?

• How's the character development? Are you convinced?

AUTHOR QUERIES:

• Who's the author?

• How's the writing?/ What do you think of the writing so far?

• Do you know anything about the author?

• Any theories about why he or she might have written this?

• How is it so far compared to his or her other books?

CRITICAL QUERIES:

Depending on the book…

• What genre is this?

• How is it so far compared with other books about _____?

• Does it feel plausible?

• How's the pace?

• What's the conflict or problem?

• What's the narrative voice? How's that working for you?

• What do you think of the dialogue/ format/style/structure/length of chapters/flashbacks and flashforwards/foreshadowing/ diction/author's experiments with _____, etc.?

WHEN IT'S A PAGE-TURNER:

• What's making this a page-turner for you, instead of a literary novel? What are you noticing about the writing?

WHEN THE TEACHER HASN'T READ THE BOOK:

• I haven't read this book yet. How is it?/What do you think of it so far?/How's the writing?

PROCESS QUERIES:

• Why did you decide to read this one?

• I can't believe how much you read last night. How come?

• You aren't 20 pages ahead of where you were yesterday. What happened last night?

• Would you call this a Holiday, Just Right, or Challenge?

• Can you follow what's happening?

• Why did you decide to reread this one?

• Where did you find this book?

WHEN THERE'S LITTLE OR NO ZONE:

• Is this book taking you into the reading zone?

• Why do you think this book is taking you so long?

• If you were going to rate this one right now, what number would you give it?

• Will you consider abandoning this one? Because if you're not hooked by now, it's more than okay to shelve it and move on.

• How many more pages will you give this book to get good before you abandon it?

• Can you skim the parts that drag— the descriptions, for example?

• Are you confused because it's hard to understand the language, or because you can't tell what's going on?

• Do you want to skim to find out what happens, or read just the ending, and then move on to a better book?

• What's on your Someday List? Let's look at it together.

• Do you know what book/author/ series I think you might like?

FINIS:

• So, thinking back, what themes or *so whats?* are emerging for you? What ideas about life come through the struggles of the main character? through the changes she undergoes? through what he learns?

• What did you think of how the author ended this one?

• How will you rate it?

• Is this one worthy of a booktalk?

• What are you planning to read next?

The online videos at scholastic.com/RZresources show Anne's check-ins with more than a dozen readers. The conversations were filmed in the spring; by this time in the school year, the kids have long since learned what to expect from Anne and how to respond when she parks alongside them with her status-of-the-class clipboard. Her approach is predictable—an open-ended question about the book or author, a comment about something she noticed, like the genre or how many pages a student inhaled the night before, or a continuation of the previous day's conversation. Unless a student has started a new book since the last time they met, she's able to pick up where they left off because it's easy to remember from one day to the next. And if she should forget, her status-of-the-class notes serve as a reminder.

In the check-ins, kids do at least half the talking. They grow comfortable with Anne's expectation that they'll speak and are accustomed to filling the spaces she makes for them to weigh in. They voice their opinions and observations without hesitation because she makes it clear there are no wrong things to say about a book or how they're reading it.

Anne relates to the kids as a more experienced reader. She's curious, enthusiastic, and knowledgeable. She shares her own strategies and preferences, and when there's a literary term to describe what a reader is noticing or feeling, she uses or teaches it in context. In the check-ins transcribed below, the critical concepts that come up include *character*, *plausibility*, *plot device*, *suspension of disbelief*, *perspective*, and *theme*. The critical vocabulary includes *memoir*, *vignette*, *cliffhanger*, *context*, *copyright*, *transitions*, and *edition*.

Caroline listens and takes notes as a kindergartener reads to her

Ted checks in with a second-grade reader

Glenn and a sixth grader discuss her favorite genre

Anne and a seventh grader compare two of an author's books

Inside the Check-In

We selected these four check-ins for transcription because they represent a range of genres, authors, and student ability levels, and because Anne hadn't read two of the books, *Are We Smart Enough to Know How Smart Animals Are?* by Frans de Waal and the fifth book in the Game of Thrones series—although she did make it all the way through the first volume, which was enough for her to get the gist of George R. R. Martin.

Ella

Ella was new to our school and reading workshop and had taken off like a rocket. Her book choice is a young adult novel that's new to the classroom library. When Anne had booktalked it the day before, she explained that its title is an allusion to Arthur Conan Doyle's first Sherlock Holmes adventure, *A Study in Scarlet*. Here she nudges Ella to move beyond her initial visceral reaction to a main character and pay attention to how the author is developing—changing—the character.

INSIDE THE READING ZONE

Check-in/Reading Conference With Ella

scholastic.com/ RZresources

Ella and *A Study in Charlotte* by Brittany Cavallaro

ANNE:	Wow, you got a big start on this last night.
ELLA:	Yeah, I did.
ANNE:	What's happening?
ELLA:	Jamie punched the—what's his name? The other…
ANNE:	Jamie?
ELLA:	Yeah, and now he's talking to Charlotte about how they're predicting that somebody's recreating this other band.
ANNE:	Right. So, what do you think about the whole concept of modernizing Sherlock Holmes?
ELLA:	I like it. I think it's really weird that they're long descendants.
ANNE:	So is that plausible to you?
ELLA:	Yeah. It's like, I don't know how that would have happened but, yeah.
ANNE:	You're willing to go with it?
ELLA:	Yeah.
ANNE:	We call that when you suspend your disbelief. You sort of say, "Okay, I'm going to go with this for the sake of the story." Is the story worth it so far?
ELLA:	Yes. I don't really like Charlotte though. She seems, I don't know, like there's something behind her maybe.
ANNE:	Maybe like more than meets the eye?

ELLA:	Yeah.
ANNE:	Interesting. It will be really interesting to see how she changes.
ELLA:	Cause I feel like she's already changing.
ANNE:	Really?
ELLA:	A little bit, yeah.
ANNE:	How so?
ELLA:	Before, she really didn't care about Jamie. But now she's talking to him more, and not keeping everything a secret.
ANNE:	So, just the fact that she's opening up to him is already changing her character?
ELLA:	Yeah!
ANNE:	That's interesting. And what page are you on?
ELLA:	Fifty-nine.
ANNE:	Great. This will be a good one for a full weekend.
ELLA:	Yeah.
ANNE:	Thanks a lot.

Joe

At Joe's previous parent-teacher-student evaluation conference, among the reading goals he set for himself was to try a memoir. Anne catches him on his second day with David Sedaris. Mostly she wants to find out if he's happy—if the choice is a good one and if he'll stay with the book.

INSIDE THE READING ZONE

Check-in/Reading Conference With Joe

scholastic.com/ RZresources

Joe and *Naked* by David Sedaris

ANNE:	So, Joe, David Sedaris?
JOE:	Yeah, I picked this up knowing it's a memoir. And at my conference, I said I was going to try one of those, so….
ANNE:	So you're working toward one of your goals?
JOE:	Yeah.
ANNE:	Did you talk to Nolan about this one?
JOE:	No, I did not. I know he picked it up a little while ago.
ANNE:	Yeah, he really likes David Sedaris. I'm a huge fan of his, too, especially the way he writes about his family. What's the first story about?

JOE:	Well, right now, he's talking about him in college with his roommate and some of the things he does that are kind of odd. It's something that normal college students wouldn't really do.
ANNE:	So, he's got a quirky roommate?
JOE:	Yeah.
ANNE:	And are you enjoying the humor? What do you think of it?
JOE:	I like the way he's writing it. I like the memoir style of writing. I didn't think it would be this fast to read.
ANNE:	He almost reminds me of the vignettes that you guys are writing for the yearbook, in terms of finding humor in the everyday.
JOE:	Yeah, they are kind of like that.
ANNE:	So, what page?
JOE:	Page 20.
ANNE:	Good start. You think you can stick with this one?
JOE:	Yeah, I'm really liking it.
ANNE:	Fun cover, too.
JOE:	Yeah.
ANNE:	Thanks, Joe.

Jolie

Jolie says she wants to be a veterinarian when she grows up. She's already the class animal rights activist. The book by Frans de Waal is a Challenge for her, but her interest keeps her hanging in there. To support Jolie, Anne offers the strategies that she uses when she finds the vocabulary in a book to be heavy going.

Jolie and *Are We Smart Enough to Know How Smart Animals Are?*
by Frans de Waal

ANNE:	So, Jolie, I have to tell you that when I ordered this book, you were the person who came into my mind. I am really glad to see that you decided to pick it up.
JOLIE:	I really like it. I learned so much in the first 40 pages.
ANNE:	So, where does he start?
JOLIE:	Well, he starts talking about ticks actually.
ANNE:	Really? That's pretty timely.

INSIDE THE READING ZONE

Check-in/Reading Conference With Jolie

scholastic.com/ RZresources

JOLIE: Yeah. So it's really interesting that ticks are eyeless and we, mammals, produce some type of acid and they can smell that acid.

ANNE: Really?

JOLIE: Yeah, and that's how they find mammals, because they can smell you coming along.

ANNE: So, it is actually less of being annoying and more of just being smart?

JOLIE: Yeah, they're pretty intelligent.

ANNE: Wow, that's interesting. Is that the first of many examples?

JOLIE: Yeah. It goes all over, kind of. It's easy to get lost. I'm on a chapter now that's talking about "Do dogs desire?" It's giving lots of other examples of mammals who *do* desire.

ANNE: How do they measure that?

JOLIE: Well…

ANNE: You'll find out?

JOLIE: Yeah, they're doing tests and stuff. Kind of sad actually. They're talking about a test they do on rats.

ANNE: Is that hard to read about?

JOLIE: Yeah, but also some Asian elephants can… like if they see their reflection in the mirror, they know it's them.

ANNE: Wow! That's very cool.

JOLIE: Yeah, but it's only *some* Asian elephants, and not with African elephants.

ANNE: That is so interesting. I've got to borrow this one over the summer.

JOLIE: Yeah, it's really cool.

ANNE: How is it in terms of nonfiction? How does it read?

JOLIE: It's good. There's a lot of advanced vocabulary.

ANNE: Can you figure it out from context?

JOLIE: Yes. There are a lot of new words though.

ANNE: Like a lot of specific vocabulary?

JOLIE: Yeah.

ANNE: If there's anything you have to look up, you can always check the dictionary. Sometimes, you know what I do, I use a sticky note as a bookmark, and I jot down things I want to look up later. Then you won't have to pull yourself out of the reading zone to go check every time there's a word.

JOLIE: I really like it. It's very interesting.

ANNE: I'm so glad you're enjoying it. It would be a great one to booktalk when you finish. What page are you on?

JOLIE: Page 40.

ANNE: Thanks, Jolie.

Lucas

Finally, Anne checks in with Lucas or, rather, settles in for the duration. Because his response style is to process his thinking out loud, meetings with Lucas take longer but are worth it, he is so reflective. He is filled up with observations about the writing of George R. R. Martin—about the structure of the novels, the character development, and the ongoing shifts in perspective. Although Martin isn't a personal favorite, Anne is interested in and enthusiastic about Lucas's ideas.

INSIDE THE READING ZONE

Check-in/Reading Conference With Lucas

scholastic.com/ RZresources

Lucas and *A Dance with Dragons* by George R. R. Martin

ANNE: So, I'm noticing, is this a new chapter? How long *are* Martin's chapters?

LUCAS: Yeah, he plays around with the chapters, which is interesting. Every chapter ends with, like, it leads to many cliffhangers. But what ends up happening is you're starting a chapter and you're like, "I really didn't want to go through the perspective of this character." Then, it gets really interesting by the end, and you're like, "I want to see this character again," but it takes another 50 pages to get back to that character. But in any case, people change titles throughout the book. So it is up to you to figure it out. Like this one particular character you would call a spy, assassin thing. She's in training, so she has to change who she is. She changes how she looks.

ANNE: How interesting.

LUCAS: Yeah.

ANNE: So how many times does Martin have her do that so far?

LUCAS: A few. She's one of the typical favorite characters.

ANNE: How do you feel about that as a reader, when you're feeling really engaged, then you have to press reset and start at a different spot with a different character?

LUCAS: You're like, "Oh, I really don't want to do this," but he's keeping you reading for the next 50 pages or so. You know? And by that time, you've lost interest in the old character because all of the characters are just as interesting.

ANNE: Well, that's good. Maybe that's his confidence in himself as an author, to hook you into something new?

LUCAS: I'd say so.

ANNE: So how long has he kept people waiting for his next book?

LUCAS: I think this is a 2013 copyright; I'm not exactly sure. My favorite quote of his is, "Every time someone asks me when my next book is coming out, I kill a Stark."

ANNE: This is a writer with a lot of confidence.

LUCAS: Yeah, but he's good, though. Something interesting is that there are two major things happening on opposite ends of the world, but they are still connected.

ANNE: So the transitions sort of remind you of the connections?

LUCAS: Kind of. It's just more and more stuff happens because it doesn't… when you go through a new character's perspective, it doesn't pick up where they left off. It goes through about the same time you went through when reading all the rest of the chapters. So, some stuff has happened and it's interesting to see what has happened.

ANNE: Oh. So it's all happening in real time?

LUCAS: Yeah.

ANNE: Interesting.

LUCAS: Which is a very strange thing, considering how in the fifth book, I've just gotten to a point where it's reached past the end of the fourth book. So the first half of the fifth book covers about as much time as the fourth book takes.

ANNE: So there's nothing set into stone, as far as the time line goes?

LUCAS: No. It's interesting to read, to try to get a sense of how it's working. I keep having to go back and see the map at the beginning of the book. It makes me jealous of those books that have the maps printed and folded, so you can pull them out and they will all be here.

ANNE: Oh, I bet someone will come out with an edition like that.

LUCAS: Yes, they need to.

ANNE: So, what page today?

LUCAS: Page 834.

ANNE: Thanks, Lucas.

A Different Kind of Scope and Sequence

Margaret Meek wrote, "For all the reading research we have financed, we are certain only that good readers pick their own way to literacy in the company of friends who encourage and sustain them and that… the enthusiasm of a trusted adult can make the difference" (1982). That's a scope and sequence that just makes sense.

Teach reading so that students feel the enthusiasm of a trusted adult when we talk with them about books. Teach so they get that we know—or know about—the books, that our questions will be useful to consider, that our advice is trustworthy. Invite every student to become part of a community of readers who get lost in the zone, one of a company of friends who encourage and sustain one another by discovering and sharing stories they love. Make the difference by observing, unburdening, and confirming them in the whispered conversations of each day's reading workshop.

> " For all the reading research we have financed, we are certain only that good readers pick their own way to literacy in the company of friends who encourage and sustain them and that …the enthusiasm of a trusted adult can make the difference. "
> — Margaret Meek

CHAPTER SIX

Writing About Reading by Anne

A fifth-grade boy writes to a buddy about a recent favorite book

I n addition to the conversations readers engage in about books, lovers of literature have an impulse to take our thinking back to the place that inspired it: the written word and the page. Analysis is as old as literature and also as contemporary. Book reviews and essays of criticism have a long history. I love reading the diaries of Virginia Woolf or the correspondence between the poets Elizabeth Bishop and Robert Lowell for the pleasure of witnessing them use writing to consider, gossip about, criticize, and admire something they've read. Today, book blogs proliferate, and communities of readers writing about the titles they've read flourish in online communities like Goodreads. I'm often surprised and touched by the degree of thoughtfulness, thoroughness, and insight in Amazon's customer reviews.

Literary criticism—which is what each of these readers is engaged in—is a way to make sense of someone else's writing and the experience of reading it. When I write about a book in one of the journals I've kept for years, it helps me sustain the pleasure of a transcendent reading experience or solve the puzzle of an unsatisfactory one. It's an opportunity to step away from the world of the story while I linger on its borders and explore the new perspective that reaching the final pages has granted me. As a critic, I can make broad, deep assessments of the author's style and themes, the growth of the characters, and the essential questions: Did I like it? Would I recommend it? Whom should I foist it on—or caution to avoid it?

It satisfies me to write my thoughts. Observations that flitted through my consciousness while reading crystalize when I put pen to paper or begin to type. In conversation I can become tongue-tied when trying to describe a book I loved or hated; often I only get across the headlines. But when I write, I have the luxury of finding the right words—pulling from my critical vocabulary and mining the depths as I describe a fuller story of my experience of a book.

My students have shown me I'm not alone in this impulse. In a check-in with Sophia, an eighth grader, I talked with her about the title she'd just finished. She gushed, "I can't wait to write my next letter-essay. It's going to be about *One Flew Over the Cuckoo's Nest*. There's so much I want to say to you and so much more I want to think about."

All readers deserve opportunities to go back into selected titles that lured them into the reading zone, step outside the zone, and consider what the author did to invite them in and keep them there. In their meta-analysis of the impact writing has on reading, researchers Steve Graham and Michael Herbert note the importance of—and the myriad benefits derived from—writing in response to literature when it's done right:

> Having students write about a text should enhance reading comprehension because it affords greater opportunities to think about ideas in a text, requires them to organize and integrate those ideas into a coherent whole, fosters explicitness, facilitates reflection, encourages personal involvement with texts, and involves students in transforming ideas into their own words. In short, writing about a text should enhance comprehension because it provides students with a tool for visibly and permanently recording, connecting, analyzing, personalizing, and manipulating key ideas in text (2010).

In reading workshop, I offer students three ways to do this: they write regular literary letter-essays, which Sophia refers to here; authentic book reviews, which we publish online; and brief end-of-trimester critiques of the best books they chose and read, a process described in Chapter 10.

Letter-Essays About Books

Letters about books are a staple of grades 3–8 reading workshops at CTL. Nancie developed them, inspired by the dialogue journals that Leslee Reed, a sixth-grade teacher, exchanged with her students about events in their lives (Staton, 1980). Ours have the particular goal of asking students to reflect on books in a back-and-forth with their teacher. Nancie wrote about this process in the first edition of *In the Middle* (1987) and continued to refine the approach over 30 years of teaching. Today my seventh and eighth graders write and make discoveries using the model she describes in the third edition of *In the Middle* (2015).

Every three weeks, the students in my class locate their marble composition notebooks, which we call a critic's journal, and choose the next title they'll critique. It must be a book they've finished, so they can fully consider theme, authorial choices, narrative voice, character development, and other literary features in the context of a complete work of literature; they also select an excerpt from the book to include, one that supports their assertions. A letter-essay is in-depth analysis, not a collection of first, or even most-of-the-way-through, impressions.

Students skim or reread the book, which is necessary to taking a critical stance, collect their impressions, and determine a direction for their critique—or, in Nancie's parlance, which we've adopted, they "write-off-the-page" (see Figure 6.1). Then they frame their criticism as a letter of at least three pages to me or a friend in the class—an authentic audience for their opinions—and receive a response that may push their thinking but always respects and expresses genuine interest in their literary analysis.

At the beginning of the year, I deliver an initial letter to each of them, which I've adapted from the one Nancie developed:

Teacher Letter to Invite Letter-Essays

Dear _____ ,

Your critic's notebook is a place for you, me, and your friends to consider books, authors, and writing. You'll think about books in informal essays directed to me and classmates, and we'll write back to you about your ideas and observations. Your letter-essays and our responses will become a record of the reading, critiquing, learning, and teaching we accomplish together.

Each of your letter-essays should be at least three pages long and written in response to one book—in other words, not a series of paragraphs about a series of books, but a long look at one title that intrigued you. You should write a letter-essay to me or a friend in your own notebook every three weeks, due on Thursday mornings. We'll correspond in cycles: you'll write two letter-essays to me, then two to one friend of your choosing, then two to me again.

Before you write a letter-essay, look back over your reading record. Which title that you finished would be enjoyable to revisit as a fan? What book you abandoned—or remained hopeful about to the bitter end—would be interesting to revisit in a slam? Once you've decided, return to the book, skim it to refresh your memory, write-off-the-page about it, and select at least one passage that you think is significant, in terms of the theme, character development, or author's style: a chunk of text you think shows something essential about how the book is written. Hand-copy or photocopy the passage you chose, include it in your letter-essay, and explain what it shows about the writing and your response to it.

What else might you do in a letter-essay? Describe what you noticed about how an author wrote. Tell about your experience as a reader of the book. Offer your opinions and pose your questions about the author, characters, plot, plausibility, or conflict. Try the paragraph openers to fuel your thinking and writing. And always tell what you think the theme or *so what?* of a book is.

Once you've written your letter-essay, hand-deliver your critic's notebook to your correspondent. If that's me, put it on my rocking chair on Thursday morning. When a friend gives you his or her notebook, you should answer in at least paragraph length by Monday morning. After you've written back, hand-deliver your friend's notebook—don't put it in his or her locker or backpack. You may not lose or damage another's notebook.

Date your letter-essays in the upper right-hand corner, and use a conventional greeting (Dear _____ ,) and closing (Love, Your friend, Sincerely). Always cite the name of the author and the book title in the first paragraph. Indicate the title by capitalizing and underlining it, e.g., The Outsiders by S. E. Hinton.

I'm already looking forward to reading and thinking about literature with you in this serious-but-friendly way. I can't wait for your first letter-essay and a year of chances to learn from you, learn with you, and help you learn more about the power and pleasures of books.

Love,

Anne

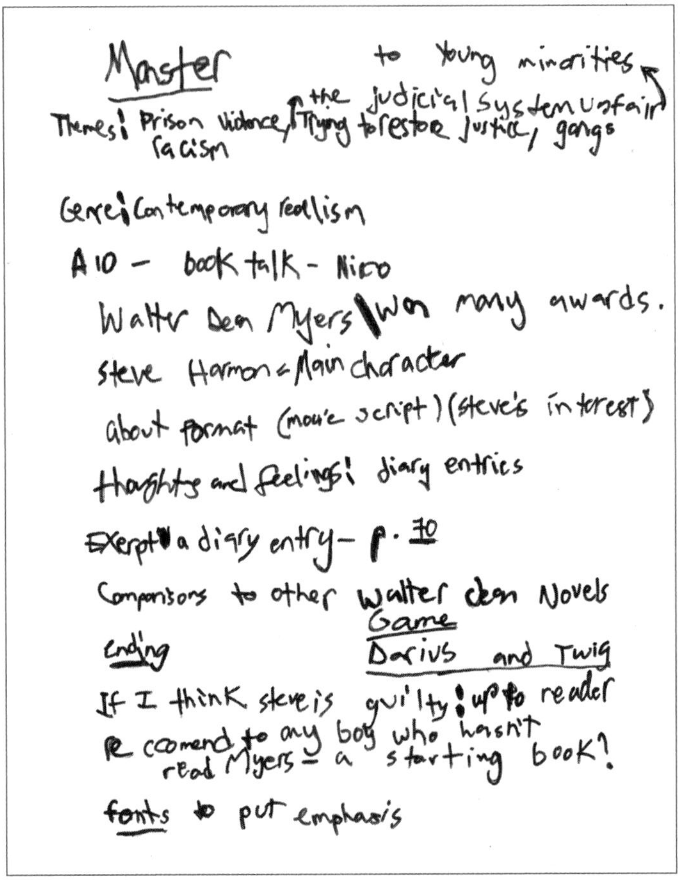

Monster

Themes: Prison violence, Trying to restore justice, the judicial system unfair to young minorities, gangs
racism

Genre: Contemporary realism

A10 - book talk - Nico

Walter Dean Myers won many awards.

Steve Harmon = Main character

about format (movie script) (Steve's interest)

thoughts and feelings: diary entries

Exerpt a diary entry - p. 70

Comparisons to other Walter dean Novels

Game

ending Darius and Twig

If I think steve is guilty: up to reader

Recomend to any boy who hasn't read Myers - a starting book!

fonts to put emphasis

FIGURE 6.1 Nolan's writing-off-the-page for a letter-essay about *Monster* by Walter Dean Myers

Then I distribute a packet of letter-essays by former students, and we read these and tease out two lists of criteria: one that details what *must* appear in a letter-essay (a discussion of theme, an excerpt identified by its page number, a formal opening and closing, the name of the author, the title of the book, etc.) and another that outlines what *might also* be included (a discussion of diction, pacing, tone, genre, narrative voice, structure, author's style, symbolism, etc.). Some kids find it helpful to refer to a list of paragraph openers when taking on the voice of a critic and transitioning from one point to the next in their letter-essays.

Writing About Reading: Some Paragraph Openers

- I was surprised when/
angry about/
moved by/
amused at/
confused when…

- Beyond its plot, I think the *theme* of this book, what it's really about, is…

- I notice how the author…

- I like/don't like the way the author…

- I don't get why the author…

- I wonder why the author…

- If I were the author, I would have…

- I wish that the author…

- I agree with/don't agree with how the author…

- I'm satisfied/dissatisfied with how the author…

- Compared with this author's other books,…

- This author's writing reminds me of…

- I think the title is…

- I think the main character's problem…

- I think the main character's thoughts and feelings or *reflections*…

- I think the main character's reaction…

- I think the character development…

- I think the way the author resolved the main character's problem…

- I think the way the main character changes shows…

- I think the supporting characters…

- The sensory details…

- The descriptions…

- The author's choice of narrative voice…

- The action…

- The dialogue…

- The setting…

- The structure of the story…

- The climax of the plot…

- The ending…

- The genre…

- This is how I read this book:…

- Next time I read a book like this, I'll…

- I rated this one _____ because…

Student Letter-Essays: Insightful Takes on Literature

The letter-essays that result are insightful takes on literature. They're valuable to me, too, for the insights they give me into what students are observing, wondering about, and responding to as critics. For example, in a letter-essay written in eighth grade, Sydney shows me she can notice how diction and cadence create lyrical prose. She knows to go back into dense or ambiguous parts of a text to consider and unpack them. She's conscious of and analytical about an author's decisions about how much information the narrator will reveal, and she reacts as a critic when a turn in plot doesn't work for her.

Dear Anne,

I hope your last week before break went well. How was Chinese New Year? Florida has been a nice and relaxing location to catch up on sleep and reading. I recently finished *The Walls Around Us* by Nova Ren Suma and loved every bit of it.

Suma managed to make every sentence and phrase meaningful and poetic. Though it was written in prose, it read like poetry. I appreciate that Suma didn't write the story in free verse, though she easily could have, because I feel that experimenting with line breaks and white space would take away from the raw beauty of the text itself. After reading many free-verse novels that sound like a prose piece hacked into poetry, it was refreshing to read a prose novel that included the cadence of poetry without overdoing it.

The plot of this book was so complex and beautifully intertwined, I felt the need to skim though it again after completing it, and I'm glad I did. I found it fascinating and ironic after knowing the ending of how Violet blamed herself for Ori's punishment. The first time through, I interpreted her guilt as remorse that she made herself an easy target for bullies, but on second thought, I wondered if she remembered how guilty she really was. I think this excerpt is an example of a paragraph with cadence, and one I interpreted differently reading it a second time.

Ori's dead because of what happened out behind the theater, in the tunnel made out of trees. She's dead because she got sent to that place upstate, locked up with those monsters. And she got sent there because of me (pp. 14–15).

I loved how the author withheld information from the reader until the very end, filling the last chapter with surprises that I didn't expect at all. It taught me to think outside the box as a reader and not to wholeheartedly believe the narrator, as she might be unreliable.

It's hard to choose one theme for this book, because I think there are so many. I think the umbrella that covers all the other aspects of this book is that guilt and innocence, polar opposites, can be easily mistaken and the consequences are immense. This is easily shown in the crime case surrounding the ballet school, and I found it remarkable how, in one sentence, Violet turned the tables.

Though, overall, I enjoyed this book, I can't help but question Suma on her use of time travel. She did a great job of tying all the loose strings together by the end of the book, except for the inexplicable conversation between future Violet and past Amber. I think that chapter completely derailed the plot from the supernatural aspects of ghosts, and instead distracted the reader from the otherwise engaging and understandable plot. The whole confusion could have easily been removed, and I don't know why it wasn't.

I would rate this book a nine (taking off a point for the time travel). I think that everyone in our class would enjoy the mystery, thrill, and intellectuality combined into a great book.

Sincerely,
Sydney

In my response, written over the weekend, I reacted to Sydney's observations about the author's language choices and tied them to an earlier conversation with her about lackluster free-verse novels. I also reinforced the concept of an *unreliable narrator*, drew her attention to the role an editor plays in the development of a book, and offered a recommendation of another title.

Anne replies to a student's letter-essay

Dear Sydney,

Thank you for this convincing critique. You're able to explore so many aspects of what made *The Walls Around Us* a stunning read. I particularly love what you wrote about Suma's lyrical prose. I, too, found it more poetic than a lot of free-verse novels, which, as you say and we've discussed in class, are really just hacked up, mediocre prose—perhaps attempts to get in on the free-verse trend in YA fiction?

I agree that withholding information from the reader is an effective literary device. The idea of the "unreliable narrator" is one I *love* but see more frequently in adult fiction than YA. I wonder if some authors think it might be too confusing for teen audiences; I like that Suma doesn't underestimate her readers.

Your critique of the novel's concluding time travel element is a valid one. It makes me wish Suma had an editor with your analytical eye to encourage her to rethink and revise it. I can see you as a pretty insightful book editor yourself someday.

Yours truly,

Anne

P.S. We have another book by N.R.S. called *Imaginary Girls* in the classroom library. Would you be interested in adding it to your Someday List?

Of course, not every student fully understands the criteria at first, or responds at Sydney's level. In Ben's first-ever letter-essay, he's able to analyze aspects of the book he chose, and even provide some evidence, but he doesn't understand yet how to incorporate a discussion of theme.

Dear Anne,

I recently finished *Shooting Star* by Frederick McKissack, Jr. I thought it was awesome. I rated it a ten.

I thought that McKissack really captured and showed the average life of an amazing high school football player. He used the character of Jayson to play a huge part in why Jomo couldn't control himself and eventually went overboard. The author never came out and said it, but I could read between the lines and see that Jomo was jealous of Jayson and how much better he was at football. I could see the envy here:

"Dude, would you go to West Point—or any of the academies?" Jomo suddenly asked.

Jayson hopped up and reached over to a small beige metal cabinet. He flipped through several file folders, pulled out two envelopes, and tossed them to Jomo. They were introductory letters from Annapolis and the Air Force Academy.

"Nah," Jayson said. "Too harsh, man. I read about the first year at these places—folks hollering and shouting, getting up at the break of dawn, and then you've got to give up four or five years after graduation. I'm down with the military, but I'm looking at the NFL, not getting shot at."

Jomo folded the Air Force Academy letter into a sleek paper airplane and sailed it out the door and into the hall. (pp. 66–67)

I know that if I were fighting for a starting spot and my best friend was getting letters, emails, and texts from colleges, I would be *very* jealous.

I thought everything about this book was well written, except for the ending. That's why I rated it a nine and not a ten. I thought McKissack crammed too much material into a limited amount of space. The pace was way too fast. The author tried to resolve Jomo's problem with his girlfriend, then he added Jomo getting ejected from his team's state championship football game and punching a reporter as he exited the stadium. To top it all off, he crashed his car while he was going home. This was all too much and too rushed for me.

I especially enjoyed reaching the "turn" of the book, or the moment when Jomo realized he was out of control. McKissack revealed it to the reader in small pieces, which made me want to read on. It started when Jomo was at football practice and he missed a hit he knew he could make. The next time the same kid ran at him, Jomo hit so hard the boy couldn't move and the coach asked Jomo to leave practice. At that moment, Jomo was conflicted because he didn't know whether that was a side effect from the performance enhancers or just his natural instinct.

Finally, I loved the change McKissack showed in Jomo. Once I finished, I could really notice the change in his attitude and self-confidence.

The genre of this book is definitely contemporary sports fiction, which is my favorite. After reading *Shooting Star*, I'm definitely going to read more by McKissack and more in this genre.

Sincerely,

Ben

I responded to Ben's first letter of seventh grade by acknowledging what he'd done well and then pushing him to consider theme, within the context of this specific book as well as all the other titles he would write about.

Dear Ben,

Thanks for your thoughtful first letter-essay. I'm looking forward to reading your ideas about books this year. McKissack's sounds like it appealed to a lot of your interests and your preferences as a reader.

I was interested to read your observations about how McKissack conveyed the dynamic between Jayson and Jomo. When you're "reading between the lines," you're making *inferences* about the jealousy that McKissack implies. And your critique of the ending sounds legitimate—it may have been a little bit *too* action packed. Do you think McKissack or his editors might believe that a teen audience needs a lot of conflict and excitement? Sometimes restraint is more effective, yes?

Ben, it's important that you remember to consider *theme* in every letter-essay. That's the crucial piece missing from your analysis of *Shooting Star*. You get close when you mention how Jomo changes. Go further and ask yourself what big lessons he learns over the course of the novel. What larger ideas or *so whats?* about life is McKissack trying to get across? For the rest of the books you write about this year, make sure you ask these kinds of questions, to get at the ideas inside the story.

Thanks, Ben.

Yours truly,

Anne

> *Letter-essays are valuable for the opportunities they give kids to comment on a range of aspects of literature.*

Letter-essays are valuable for the opportunities they give kids to comment on a range of aspects of literature. Over the course of a whole year of reading and writing, they touch on a wide variety of literary features. Nolan went deep in considering the language used by Roland Smith in his letter-essay about *The Edge*:

The feature I was most impressed with in this novel was Smith's sensory diction. I believed in his description of Afghanistan's mountain landscapes: It's rugged and spare, but it has its own stark beauty. I look forward to getting down there to feel the rock under my feet and hands and smell the dust and dirt in the cool mountain air. I love how Smith uses three different senses in just a few lines of description: sight, touch, and smell.

Nolan's classmate Hope used a letter-essay to think on paper about symbolism, in response to *The Fifth Wave* by Rick Yancey.

> I liked how Yancey added ongoing symbols, like the one used throughout the series of the silver chain. For Ben, the chain is literal and also a metaphor because of his sister's locket that he carries around with him after she is killed. Yancey uses it in different parts of the novel to make readers think about how all the characters and events are connected like links in the chain.

Maintaining a critic's journal also allows students to draw upon a whole year's worth of reading to make comparative analyses, as Nicco did in his letter about the influence of a George Orwell classic:

> One specific genre that I've noticed become increasingly popular is a dystopian novel where the government gets too much power. That concept stems directly from *1984*. The book I'm currently reading, *The Circle* by Dave Eggers, is a variation on this theme: the out-of-control authority figure, in this case with a company. *1984* is a timeless classic, and, in my opinion, it's because it's about a subject that will always be relevant, regardless of the time period: what if an institution got out of control and took over the lives of citizens?

…they enjoy a richer experience when their literary criticism is a social interaction, as well—when they correspond with a peer about a book.

The Pleasures of Peer Correspondence

As much as students appreciate receiving a response from me, they enjoy a richer experience when their literary criticism is a social interaction, as well—when they correspond with a peer about a book. After two letter-essays to me, kids choose a classmate to receive and respond to their next two, before cycling back to me, and so on. Eventually I get to read all the letter-essays, regardless of the audience. I love the inside jokes, nicknames, and exuberance that emerge when middle schoolers write to one another.

A third grader writes a lit letter to a classmate

When Amelia wrote to her friend Sophia about *The Scarlet Pimpernel*, she took on the tone and diction that the author, Emma Orczy, uses to describe life in France during the Revolution. Amelia totally committed to her bit—the letter was handwritten in ornate cursive—while still including the elements of an effective literary critique.

Dear Lady Sophia,

This time I will inform you of my most favorite old book. It goes by the title of *The Scarlet Pimpernel*—a classic, skillfully crafted by the Baroness Orczy. It was excellent, but my overall review only resulted in a well-earned nine, for reasons I shall reveal later.

My copy of the book is ancient. It is in tatters, but obviously because it was so lovingly read by so many. It has gained the smell often associated with old books from countless years spent on a library shelf.

But enough about the physical remains of this priceless jewel. I will now give you a taste of the elaborate story within: one filled with daring journeys taken to save loved ones in danger during the bloodthirsty times of the French Revolution.

The language is somewhat flowery, causing me to skim along whole paragraphs at times, but that did not interrupt the plotline. However, that is the one reason its ranking is a nine, not a ten or a "Bella."

Still, Baroness Orczy is able to incorporate enough sensory diction to interest the reader. In the passage below I've underlined examples:

She had not been in Paris for some months; the <u>horrors</u> and <u>bloodshed</u> of the <u>Reign of Terror, culminating</u> in the September <u>massacres</u>, had only come across the Channel to her as a <u>faint echo</u>. Robespierre, Danton, Marat, she had not known in their new guise of <u>bloody justiciaries, merciless wielders of the guillotine.</u> Her very soul <u>recoiled in horror</u> from these excesses, to which she feared her brother Armand—moderate republican as he was—might become one day the <u>holocaust</u> (p. 87).

The all-encompassing theme was somewhat difficult for me to draw out from between the pages at first. But my end result is this: along the way, you may distance yourself from the one you truly love, the one who faithfully loves you back, but the passion, no matter how dormant, will live on and resurface at the most unexpected of times. Therefore, dear Lady, you must always be cognizant of its existence, so when it awakens, it will not be like a hard blow to the cheek.

In other words: love never dies and will again reveal itself at the most needed hour.

My Lady, congratulations on your acceptance into CHS. I send the best of wishes your way. If you choose to attend, I hope that your time there will be full of outstanding memories and lasting friendships.

Yours truly,
Comtesse de Genus de Mingori

Dearest Amelia,

I would agree with your assessment—the excerpt you gave was verbose. I can understand why you gave the novel a nine.

Out of curiosity, what year was this book written? The diction you noted seemed difficult to understand at times. This novel would definitely be a challenge for me. I think you should booktalk this one. It would be interesting to know how others might react to the complex language—and theme. It seemed like you were able to draw it out quite well.

I was very impressed by the strong vocabulary choices you made in your letter. Good job!

Thank you for your kind words about high school. I hope that both of us may be led on the right path and make decisions that only result in positive futures.

Lots of love,
Sophia

Developing Identities as Readers and Critics

The growth in thinking that my students' letter-essays demonstrate is, to me, remarkable. Plus there's nothing that compares to a critic's journal as a thorough record of a student's responses to literature over the course of a school year—or two, in my case, since I teach readers for seventh and eighth grades and request that they use the same marble notebook both years. Over the course of the pages of one critic's journal, kids move from plot-heavy summaries of light young adult novels to nuanced criticisms of such books as *The Poisonwood Bible* by Barbara Kingsolver, Orwell's *Animal Farm*, and Heller's *Catch-22*. Their analyses of theme deepen; their chosen excerpts are increasingly focused and relevant. At a time when teachers are hungry for authentic documentation of student growth, this simple journal speaks volumes. It *is* the record—and a treasure. It also lays some important groundwork.

We know that in high school and college English courses, much of the writing our kids will be asked to produce is literary analysis. The critical thinking of the letter-essays prepares kids for this assignment in a friendly way. With a few tweaks in format, the letters could become formal essays. In addition, my students grow comfortable with planning a written analysis of literature and using a critical lexicon. While the letters allow room to experiment and to incorporate voice, they also hold their own as essays of literary criticism for the middle-school level. This makes them the perfect bridge to English in high school and beyond.

It's also a fulfilling process for middle schoolers. Developing a level of comfort with literary criticism—in a social way that they enjoy—builds confidence as well as skills of analysis. And the letters allow kids to develop identities as readers and critics.

> " *At a time when teachers are hungry for authentic documentation of student growth, this simple journal speaks volumes. It is the record—and a treasure.* "

Book Reviews

Another way my students write about their reading is in book reviews, a writing workshop genre study that Nancie developed and outlines in the third edition of *In the Middle*. Unlike the school genre of book reports, reviews are a valuable and widespread venue for criticism in the adult world. This becomes clear to my students whenever I give them copies of reviews from *The New York Times Book Review* and *VOYA* magazine, so they can vote on titles for me to purchase for the classroom library.

By the time they write reviews, usually after the winter holidays, kids have become accustomed to writing about their reading in letter-essays. We launch the genre study by reading examples of professional and student reviews; then the class teases out a list of differences and similarities. In general, they agree that their own reviews should provide a brief plot synopsis, enough to intrigue a reader without revealing too much; begin with a crafted lead that draws a reader in; conclude deliberately; provide the details—author, publisher, number of pages; and urge a reader of the review in one direction or the other regarding the book.

As with their letter-essays, students select a book they've finished and go back into it—skim or reread it—in order to plan their reviews. They write-off-the-page, and then draft, revise, edit, polish, and publish. And they reach authentic prospective readers who are curious about the books, both in our class and beyond it.

First I photocopy and collate an anthology, a class set of the reviews, and schedule a reading. Students pore through the reviews with their Someday Lists beside them and cups of cocoa in hand. As they read their peers' endorsements, they jot down the titles they want to read someday.

Next I post the reviews on CTL's book blog, "You Gotta Read This!" The blog, which can be browsed by genre and searched according to title or author, is, along with the book lists in the "Kids Recommend" section, the most frequently visited page on the CTL website (c-t-l.org). My students love knowing that their recommendations are influencing the contents of other classroom libraries. And I value the additional insights the reviews afford me into what they're understanding as readers and able to express as critics. As Graham and Herbert explain, "Transforming a mental summary of text into writing requires additional thought about the essence of the material, and the permanence of writing creates an external record of this synopsis that can be readily critiqued" (2010). Book reviews are yet another way that students' writing about literature informs my work as a teacher of individual readers.

In his review of *The Circle* by Dave Eggers, eighth grader Noah opens with an intriguing lead, provides a concise plot synopsis, offers some personal analysis and an

The Circle by Dave Eggers

Reviewed by Noah Jordan

Exploring a scenario not too distant from reality, Dave Eggers has written a dystopian novel that questions the extent to which technology has taken over our society. In this book, The Circle is the Earth's most powerful Internet company. Based in California, its slogan is "All that happens must be known."

A young woman named Mae Holland gets a job there, meeting up with her best friend, Annie. Mae takes a tour of the campus and views The Circle: beautiful glass buildings, outdoor swimming pools, tanks of rare deep-sea fish, and almost anything else you can imagine. It seems perfect. When The Circle reveals a miniature surveillance camera that's almost unnoticeable and can wirelessly stream to a larger screen anywhere in the world, it seems harmless. But is this new type of technology threatening society's privacy? The short answer is yes.

Eggers tells a thrilling story of how technology can change our lives for better and for worse. He brilliantly describes the many ways it changes Mae's life—personally and socially—and the many ways she wishes she could stay the same. He describes how her relationship with Annie changes, how her personality changes, and how stress devours her everyday life. The Circle takes the reader on a fantastic journey through life in a technology-run world.

Eggers explores the fact that in our world, spying creates tension throughout society, but describes it through a fictional scenario. When reading this novel, I couldn't help but think of current issues, such as the National Security Agency spying on civilians. Eggers wrote in a way that I can see Mae change, Annie change, and The Circle change, all because of a small creation that originated in a simple thought: all that happens must be known.

The Circle is a wonderful book that opens up all sorts of questions about modern technology. I would recommend it to anyone who's open to understanding the drawbacks to "advances" in society.

Alfred A. Knopf, 491 pages

overview of the novel's themes, connects the book to current events, and concludes with a recommendation about which audience of readers might appreciate it.

This kind of writing is valuable—to the writer, to the reader, to the teacher—and satisfying. After they've enjoyed getting lost in the world of a story, kids emerge from the reading zone with a sense of nourishment and companionship, bringing friends and teacher into the worlds they inhabited vicariously, learning how to notice and name how literature works.

Writing about reading in these two ways feels authentic and productive. Each gives my students a sense of autonomy because, whether it's the subject of a letter-essay or a review, they choose the book. They also select their own entry points: there's no prescribed prompt. And, in the case of the letter-essays, they decide on their peer correspondents during the cycles when that's not me. Those questions—What book do I want to revisit as a critic? What will I decide to explore about it? Whom will I share my thoughts with?—invite excitement and engagement, as opposed to more typical feelings of dread, boredom, and obligation about assigned lit-crit essays or book reports.

> *...kids emerge from the reading zone with a sense of nourishment and companionship, bringing friends and teacher into the worlds they inhabited vicariously, learning how to notice and name how literature works.*

Rewards of Original Thinking

As their teacher, I feel excited to read my students' opinions about books. I know I'm going to be responding to original thinking—kids' own insights—instead of a class set of essays that make the same essential points about a class novel, informed by class discussions that I led. Instead, because each student is analyzing a different book, their responses are diverse, fresh, voiced, and unique to them as critics. Writing about reading has always been, at its best, a rewarding intellectual endeavor. Our students deserve to experience it that way.

CHAPTER SEVEN

Discussion and Close Reading

Anne's kids unpack and discuss a daily poem

Since my students all chose and read different books, a significant element was missing from my teaching and their learning: opportunities for whole-group discussion. To remedy that, I began to launch each class with a poem, as an occasion for a collaborative exploration of a work of literature, but also because it was the best ritual I could imagine.

Poetry is the essential genre. The lessons it teaches about good writing, critical reading, the kinds of adults adolescents wish to become, and the kind of world they hope to inhabit extend a beguiling invitation to kids to grow up literate, healthy, and whole. Wallace Stevens wrote that the poet's role is "to help people live their lives" (1951). A poem a day helps students begin to lead lives of worth.

> *A poem a day helps students begin to lead lives of worth.*

Because it is a poem, it takes about 10 minutes to read and talk about it. The compactness of the genre makes it possible for the class to enjoy a shared encounter with literature and develop critical eyes, critical ears, and a vocabulary for discussing literary features without robbing them of the time and autonomy they need to grow as independent readers.

At the end of a trimester, when they assess their work as readers and critics (see Chapter 10), each student looks back, decides which were the best poems of the previous 12 weeks, and writes about what makes them effective. For years I kept a running list of the titles they nominated and in 2006 published a teaching anthology, *Naming the World: A Year of Poems and Lessons.*

In the lessons that accompany each poem in the book, I tease out some of the critical features teachers might make kids aware of, and I suggest a response task, a focus for students to take when they read the poem on their own and annotate it prior to a discussion. I might ask them to mark sensory verbs, the most important lines, lines they wish they'd written, lines they can see, or lines that ring true to their own experience. I varied the approach because I wanted to make the response process as fresh, lively, and unpredictable as the poems themselves. And then I had second thoughts.

I began to question whether students should have to wait for the teacher to assign the critical stance to assume with a poem. The practice made them dependent on me as unpackers of poetry, plus I wasn't convinced it was building sufficient habits of mind or observation to bring to independent experiences of poetry in high school (perhaps) and college (definitely). In addition, I taught a lot of mini-lessons about poetic features, and our daily discussions generated even more knowledge and vocabulary. I wondered if I could introduce one generous approach to unpacking poetry and then trust kids to analyze and annotate a poem on their own before we came together to discuss it. So I went back to the drawing board.

Genre Study of Free-Verse Poetry

Today, Anne's students begin the school year with a genre study of free-verse poetry, as do CTL kids in grades 1–6. They learn how to read it, critique it, and, in writing workshop, craft it (Atwell, 2015). Every lesson that matters about effective writing—except paragraphing, although stanza breaks come pretty close, function-wise—can be highlighted easily in free verse. And because of the compactness of the genre, every seventh and eighth grader finishes two or three pieces of writing by the end of September and experiences a complete writing process that many times. From the lessons that poetry teaches them about purpose and craft, kids begin to understand that writers of every genre observe, select, shape ideas, identify feelings, and communicate with real readers. Along the way, they learn the basics of drafting, revising, and editing, and they participate in a couple of lovely readings of class anthologies of their poems.

At the same time, during reading workshop, Anne introduces, reinforces, and asks students to practice a process for reading and annotating poems on their own. It is informed by her mini-lessons, a glossary of poetic terms she introduces (Appendix A), and a set of questions I developed the last year I taught, which she asks them to consider each time they respond to a poem.

Unpacking a Poem
Some Considerations When You Annotate

- What do you notice about how the poem is written? What do you like? (Think pattern, form, diction, images, details, figurative language, sound effects, surprises, title, conclusion.)

- What's happening, literally, in the poem? Do any words or lines confuse you?

- How does the poem make you feel? Which words or lines make you feel that way?

- Which lines do you think are the most important?

- Does anything in the poem remind you of another poem, poet, or writer?

- What themes—ideas about life—emerge from the poem?

Online we've posted two poetry discussions filmed in Anne's reading workshop (at scholastic.com/RZresources). Each follows the predictable routine she establishes the first week of school. She distributes copies of a poem and creates a context for it, some combination of the social, cultural, personal, literary, or historical. Then she reads it with as much nuance as she can bring to its form and diction, so students can ride on her voice into the world of the poem and begin to hear and see its structure and meaning.

Next, she asks them to go back into the poem on their own, read it, and mark it up guided by the questions in "Unpacking a Poem." In the discussion that follows, most of the questions she poses are open ended, and many of the comments her students make are cued by their annotations. Finally, she offers a benediction—a suggestion of something for students to think about, write about, or try to be that's inspired by the poem and its themes. Along the way, Anne and her kids break just about every rule of close reading as defined in the Common Core standards.

And the kids more than benefit. After they leave us, they excel—many become valedictorians and salutatorians of their high school classes; their college acceptances include Amherst, Bowdoin, Dartmouth, Harvard, Middlebury, Williams, and Stanford. Wherever they go next, they are avid participants in discussions, individuals who express opinions, offer interpretations, and back up both with evidence, students who can be counted on to fill the cricket-chirping pause that follows a teacher's question. I was startled one afternoon when a local high school English teacher fell to his knees in front of me as I was wheeling through the supermarket. "Please," he begged, laughing, "send me some more of them. They talk. And what they say is so smart and pertinent."

A Brief History of Close Reading

Close reading as it's practiced at CTL—what we refer to as *unpacking a poem*—is a very different approach from the version described by the authors of the Common Core ELA standards (2011) and publishers' criteria (2012). That method in action is available to view online. One model lesson (Part 6 of usny.nysed.gov/rttt/resources/bringing-the-common-core-to-life-download.html) addresses "Letter from a Birmingham Jail" by Martin Luther King, Jr. Another demonstrates a week of lessons to a fifth-grade class about a memoir by the scientist Richard Feynman that appeared in *Cricket* magazine (commoncore.americaachieves.org/samplevideo/4f97468426b615af6b000001). If you watch them, here's what you'll see:

- Lessons, not discussions, that are "entirely teacher-directed, usually in the traditional question-reply-evaluate model," with one correct answer to almost every question (Newkirk, 2016)
- No introduction to the text—no provision of context or information about the author; no eliciting of student interest, knowledge, or experience
- Text-dependent analysis based on a formula that mandates that 80–90% of teacher questions refer back to information in the text and stay within "the four corners of the text" because "drawing knowledge from the text itself is the point of reading"
- Sentence-by-sentence analysis of the text and its vocabulary, which consumes an inordinate amount of class time: 11 40-minute sessions for "Letter from a Birmingham Jail" and five for Feynman's 1,400-word personal essay
- A teacher who does most of the talking
- Zero student response that originates with students
- Little acknowledgment of the values inherent in the text—of the implications about justice and compassion in the first or a sense of humor and sense of wonder in the second

Common Core close reading is based on the tenets of a literary movement called the New Criticism; its heyday was roughly the 1930s through 1960s. New Criticism developed as a reaction against the prevalent critical approach to poetry, which was biographical. The New Critics rejected any mode of response that was extrinsic to the text, including information about the poet's life, consideration of the historical or cultural context of the poem, and the ideas, feelings, and associations that arise when an individual reader reads the poem. They theorized that a poem must be read "objectively," as a self-contained object with only intrinsic qualities, such as structure or patterns of imagery. It's worth noting that this approach was developed and intended as a way to respond to poems, not to letters, memoirs, or other prose genres.

Eventually, a strict interpretation of New Criticism fell out of favor among most academics, who viewed it as limited, limiting, and cut off from history, as well as insufficiently concerned with the moral implications of a text. By the time I was an English major in the 1970s, our professors did ask us to analyze and annotate poems—to unpack them as close readers. But they also asked us what we noticed and thought about them, and they introduced information about the poets' lives and times. When we read and discussed poems by Gwendolyn Brooks, Countee Cullen, and Langston Hughes, it was in the context of their life stories, the Great Black Migration, Jim Crow, the Harlem Renaissance, and the Civil Rights Movement, along with our own beliefs and experiences. The readings and my responses were deeper, richer, and more memorable for it.

Fast-forward almost 50 years. Under the influence of the authors of the Common Core State Standards and assessments, New Criticism–inspired close reading has become *the* mode of reading and responding for millions of American schoolchildren and their teachers. Students are taught to inspect a text and extract the meaning instead of how to navigate a text, voice their observations and responses, and discern and discuss meanings.

Anne and I wish to make the case for an integrated approach to reading workshop, one that uses the analytical tools of New Critics to annotate and unpack the effects that readers notice—and to plumb meaning. Readers can do both things: react and relate to and interpret literature, *and* analyze how it works. Our students view poems through a critical lens "handed over" (Bruner, 1986) by the teacher in the form of a lexicon that explicates poetic features. Students who know the language can function as critics; we've found that they *do* function as critics when they have opportunities to engage together with rich, enticing texts. The poems that CTL teachers select for their classes to unpack and discuss are rich and enticing in their diction, imagery, and, especially, themes.

In September, to teach her kids the vocabulary that critics use to analyze poetry, Anne gives them copies of What We Talk About When We Talk About Poetry (Appendix A) and asks them to take it home and mark it up: draw a smiling face next to every term they already know, a frowning face next to any they don't know yet, and a question mark next to any whose definition they don't understand.

As the next day's mini-lesson, the kids discuss their question marks. Students have several days to study the lexicon and try to learn any unfamiliar terms before they have a "retrieval practice"—an ungraded, fill-in-the-blank review, which they correct themselves in a class discussion. Anne may ask her kids to review the lexicon several more times, until they feel confident about most of the vocabulary. At the same time, whenever a term comes up in relation to a daily poem, she reinforces its meaning.

Apart from the story grammar that her students learn one term at a time in the context of booktalks and mini-lessons (Chapter 4), this is the only formal vocabulary study of the school year. It's important because it gives everyone a common, accurate critical vocabulary, and it levels the playing field. By June, after a full school year of identifying poetic features in context and appreciating how poets have used them, students know them cold. They carry this knowledge with them to their high school and college English classes.

As the two posted discussions show, Anne leads them but in directions determined mostly by students. In helping them unpack the poems "Miracles" by Walt Whitman

(Figure 7.1) and "shreds of grass" (Figure 7.2) by CTL alum Avery Genus, she poses open-ended questions that get kids thinking and speaking: *What did you notice? What are your observations? Any favorites—lines you like? What did you like about it? How do you feel about this? What do you think of that? What else do you think the poet could have said? What are other people's takes on that? Any examples? Other thoughts? Other ideas to add to that one?*

In response to student contributions, Anne paraphrases or rephrases a comment, clarifies it, puts a spin on it, or compliments it with an "Interesting" or "Well said." Her whole affect demonstrates eagerness to hear what they have to say and engagement with their insights. Who wouldn't feel comfortable speaking up in this classroom?

Every student can speak up because no matter how shy or self-conscious, no matter how able or experienced, they all have something to say. Their annotations on the poems prompt their remarks, and since their notes are based on the suggestions in "Unpacking a Poem," the comments are specific and original.

When Anne does ask a close-ended question, it's because she wants to teach or reinforce a term. There are a handful of these queries: *What do you call this kind of repetition? Any thoughts on the title—on what it might be a reference to? What type of figurative language is that? What do you call it when a poem refers to another poet's writing?*

The kids show her well how they're getting their minds and mouths around the language of criticism. In the filmed discussions, the critical vocabulary includes *allusion, anaphora, annotate, cliché, concision, connotation, conclusion, diction, figurative language, homage, image, mood, personification, reference, repetition, simile, sensory verb, stanza, structure, syntax, theme,* and *tone.*

Anne provides a deliberate introduction to each poem. In fact, she speaks from notes she made the night before, as I used to do. In our experience as English teachers, students are interested in—even motivated by—background information. More significantly, we recognize that "cold" close readings (Snow, 2013) are neither fair nor productive. To an English teacher who loves literature, a big part of the job is to make the difficult doable—to anticipate and alleviate frustration and build frames of reference kids can lean on as critics of this poem today and then of all the poems still to come.

An eighth grader annotates the daily poem

Miracles

Why, who makes much of a miracle?
As to me I know of nothing else but miracles,
Whether I walk the streets of Manhattan,
Or dart my sight over the roofs of houses toward the sky,
Or wade with naked feet along the beach just in the edge
  of the water,
Or stand under trees in the woods,
Or talk by day with any one I love, or sleep in the bed at
  night with any one I love,
Or sit at table at dinner with the rest,
Or look at strangers opposite me riding in the car,
Or watch honey-bees busy around the hive of a summer
  forenoon,
Or animals feeding in the fields,
Or birds, or the wonderfulness of insects in the air,
Or the wonderfulness of the sundown, or of stars shining
  so quiet and bright,
Or the exquisite delicate thin curve of the new moon in
  spring;
These with the rest, one and all, are to me miracles,
The whole referring, yet each distinct and in its place.

To me every hour of the light and dark is a miracle,
Every cubic inch of space is a miracle,
Every square yard of the surface of the earth is spread with
  the same,
Every foot of the interior swarms with the same.

To me the sea is a continual miracle,
The fishes that swim—the rocks—the motion of the
  waves—the ships with men in them,
What stranger miracles are there?

        —Walt Whitman

FIGURE 7.1 "Miracles" by Walt Whitman

shreds of grass

on the concrete divider
bleak with shreds of grass
stood the man

battered cardboard
chest-high raised
and plea scratched
in black marker

and connection briefer was
than the gasp of a dying candle
but in that fraction
tangible the grief
in the oceans of his eyes

and as along we rolled
i stared and was ashamed
to be one of them
that passed

      —Avery Genus

FIGURE 7.2 "shreds of grass"
by Avery Genus

Anne begins her introduction to "Miracles" by drawing a line between Whitman and the Transcendentalists, whom her kids learned about on a field trip to Concord, Massachusetts, and Walden Pond. She also reminds the eighth graders that they studied Whitman the previous year; sums up his style and significance in American letters; tells about Emerson's role in the ultimate success of *Leaves of Grass*; and lets them know that although Walt wasn't an official member of "the Walden crew," he was influenced by and admired the Transcendentalists, as the "values, worldview, and philosophy" expressed in "Miracles" will make clear. She gives her students multiple ways in. Before she reads the poem—with expression and pleasure—they are already on board.

With Avery's poem, Anne establishes a personal context. After she relates it to the theme of consideration and reconsideration that has threaded through recent poems they've discussed, she explains that a reason "shreds of grass" resonates for her is the homeless, jobless people she encounters at intersections on her daily commute through Portland. She wonders if any of the students have experienced this "moment of discomfort and uneasiness," and she tells them "Avery, whom you know" did, and he used a poem to capture the moment and consider his feelings about it. When her kids enter the world of the poem with her, they do so with visual images of characters and setting, which help them to navigate Avery's unorthodox diction and syntax.

Near the end of the discussion, Anne commits an *intentional fallacy* (Wimsatt and Beardsley, 1954), a cardinal sin in New Criticism theory. After students discuss whether the title "shreds of grass" refers to "Leaves of Grass," she tells them yes, it does, and, further, "This is deliberate on Avery's part." Because Anne provides information instead of withholding her knowledge of the poet's intentions, she clears the air for her student Lucas to voice an essential theme: the contrast between Whitman's vision of the interconnectedness of all things and Avery's shame about not connecting with the homeless man. As Lucas puts it, "The title gives the poem a layer."

Some of my favorite responses to the two poems venture far beyond the four corners of the text—when Kaleb says he can feel what Avery felt, his pity and guilt, in the phrase "the gasp of a dying candle," and when Hope says she can visualize the image, too, but also when she comments, about "Miracles," "Oh, it's *very* Transcendental." I lean in when Ella and Katie identify favorite lines and tell why they like them; when Nolan tells how the word *bleak* really gets to him; when Lucas thinks out loud about how the cliché "the miracle of life" probably wasn't a cliché when Whitman and the Walden crew wrote about it because they were the first to express it. The responses show that students are taking the poems into their lives, just as Anne hoped would happen when she chose them to read and discuss.

Kids spend enough time with a poem to enter it, walk around inside it, and notice what they can about how it's made and how it affects them, which leaves plenty of class time for independent reading, still and always the essential activity. No one, student or teacher, has to endure the tedium of a microscopic analysis that kills the pleasure and meaning of a poem.

In Anne's close-reading discussions, the proportion of teacher talk to contributions from kids is significant—I reckon it's one-third Anne to two-thirds students. Alfie Kohn has written, "In outstanding classrooms, teachers do more listening than talking, and students do more talking than listening. Terrific teachers often have teeth marks on their tongues" (2015). I don't know how often Anne has to bite her tongue. I do know that she trusts kids, and she teaches her own what they might notice and what critics call it. While the text is the focus of a discussion, her students set an agenda that engages their interest, explores their reactions, *and* demonstrates their comprehension and critical chops.

> *In outstanding classrooms, teachers do more listening than talking, and students do more talking than listening. Terrific teachers often have teeth marks on their tongues.*
> —Alfie Kohn

Theme Is Essential

Our greatest concern about the other kind of close reading is its deemphasis of the core value in reading literature in the first place: *theme*, and how it resonates in our real lives. While student immersion in the reading zone happens mostly via characters and stories, the ideas they glean there inspire them to consider the complexities of the world around them and their selves in relation to it. For adolescents, theme is paramount—it fuels their attraction to literature. Because poetry explores a dynamic mix of human experiences, themes constantly tug at their minds as students read and discuss it. But the Common Core hammers home one and only one purpose for reading: to *extract*, *gather*, and *acquire knowledge*, *information*, and *evidence* (Newkirk, 2016).

Anne reinforces the themes of poems through the benedictions that signal the end of a discussion. These mostly take the form of suggestions with real-world applications—things kids might do to live the values that the poems imply.

When the class has finished unpacking Whitman's "Miracles," Anne reminds them of the Transcendentalist vision of the divine, which resides not in Heaven but inside each human and all of nature. She points out a series of rich connections—Emerson to Whitman, to American free-verse poetry, to the kids themselves and their time in Concord, to their sampling of Emerson and Thoreau, to the natural world that surrounds them. "You're a part of a tradition," she concludes. "I encourage you today, when you go outside (at recess), to consider the miracles around you, 'each distinct and in its place.'"

As the benediction to Avery's "shreds of grass," Anne reminds students that poetry is a tool they can use to explore their lives, including going back to a troubling moment and reconsidering it. She quotes the poet Adrienne Rich—"The moment of change is the only poem" (1971)—and tells them, "Sometimes that moment of change is inside yourself. Think of the moments of change in your own life and how they could become poems."

In the Territories section of their writing-reading handbooks, where kids keep track of ideas for pieces of writing (Atwell, 2015), there's a page that they've headed "Poetry Inspirations." When a poetry discussion inspires an idea to draft as a poem in writing workshop, a student can capture it here.

Unpacking: Close Reading With Heart

A discussion of a work of literature should honor the text *plus* the writer who created it, the particular context in which it was created, the reactions of students to it, and its impact on them. Literature isn't neutral. The study of literature isn't an objective science. Teachers should never feel compelled to ignore the values—implicit or explicit—conveyed by poems and stories (Rosenblatt, 1995).

Unpacking—the version of close reading that I taught, that Anne teaches—attends to words, lines, patterns, and devices without killing a child's love of poetry. It is informed, authentic, voiced, and generative. Really, it is just good old-fashioned English teaching—the kind of engaged discussion we enjoyed as students back in the day, the kind of talk that drew us to English teaching in the first place.

Fiction and Non-

In reading workshop, a third grader enjoys a storybook about dinosaurs

My daughter grew up on an island off the Maine coast—a beautiful world but a small one. The hundreds of stories her dad and I read to Anne and, later, those she read to herself enlarged both the girl and her world.

There aren't any traffic lights on the island, but when we crossed our road, three-year-old Anne informed me, "The red light says stop, and the green light says go" (a line from the book *Bathwater's Hot* by Shirley Hughes). She had never eaten in a Chinese restaurant, but Mercer Mayer's critters do in *Just Grandpa and Me*. One morning she pilfered two cinnamon sticks from my spice cabinet and explained, "These are my chopsticks." No one we know plays the accordion, which didn't stop her from rolling her toy piano on its side, heaving it up, clasping it against her chest, and staggering around the house announcing, "Look at my 'ccordian. I'm playing the 'ccordian like Rosa," the main character in *Something Special for Me* by Vera B. Williams. With help from Shirley Hughes's *Alfie's Feet*, she taught herself left from right and how to put on her boots.

A rich diet of stories entertained Anne, and they intrigued her. But stories also introduced her to other lives and cultures. They taught her new vocabulary and concepts, and because they engendered feelings and sensations, stories gave her *reasons* to remember them. Anne's knowledge of the wide world grew as she enjoyed vicarious adventures with fictional characters who engaged her imagination.

A False Dichotomy

Today, Anne and I are both, for a host of reasons, troubled by the reading criteria spelled out in the Common Core. Near the top of our list of concerns is the privileging of informational text over story. The Common Core calls for an ultimate balance of 70 percent nonfiction to 30 percent fiction in a child's school experience as a reader (Coleman and Pimental, 2012). When the authors opine that in order to be "college and career ready" students need to move away from narrative and focus on facts, they bypass a wealth of research about child development, reading development, and the influence of stories on both. It doesn't take much reading between the lines to understand that fiction is regarded as nonessential, impractical, frivolous even. This is a stunted vision both of academic standards for literacy and the language arts themselves.

There are facts and ideas in works of fiction, and they aren't trivial. Fiction addresses all of life, its myriad stages, conditions, times, and places. It explores what it means to be human and alive on the planet from all kinds of perspectives. And it is rooted in reality.

A writer of fiction has to convince a reader to buy into an invented world and believe in it until the last page. So novelists tap their own knowledge and experience, and they conduct research—about settings, characters, events, and phenomena—so the fictional world is perceivable and conceivable. A novel is not a daydream on paper.

Anne's students understand this because they write fiction, read it, and think, talk, and write about it. They recognize its power to inform and inspire as well as entertain. When she and I asked them if a novel has ever been *of use* as they consider the real world around them, every one of them said *yes*. Her seventh and eighth graders wrote for us in response to two questions: *Think about the novels you've read recently: While living inside each story, did you pick up any knowledge along the way? What did you learn about?*

Graham, a seventh grader new to our school and reading workshop, wrote about Michael Crichton's thriller *Jurassic Park*.

I discovered how much we've learned about dinosaurs since 1990 and how correct, and also incorrect, Crichton's sources and ideas were. For example, he wrote that the carnotaurus camouflaged itself and stood still all day. But it didn't. It was actually one of the most active, fastest dinosaurs.

Also, I'd always thought dinosaurs were giant, scaly lizards. Crichton thought they were more like birds but still leathery. Because of his novel's inspiration, I looked up modern paleontology and learned that we know now that dinosaurs were mostly covered with feathers, fluff, and quills. *Birds,* in other words.

I remember a day in September when Graham was so wrapped up in *Jurassic Park* he took the book outside at recess and read it instead of joining his friends in the customary game of touch football. Why? He was dying to know *what happens next.* Crichton's plot compelled him and, in its grip, so did paleontology.

The diversity and specificity of the rest of the kids' answers are a powerful rebuttal to assumptions implicit in the Common Core downgrading of fiction. Without a history textbook, science textbook, or Wikipedia entry in sight, students described insights they gleaned from fiction about the invention of baseball, life in the Jim Crow South, autism, climate change, manatees, the firebombing of Dresden and the siege of Leningrad, physical disabilities, cloning, world religions, leukemia, the conditions of slavery, censorship, the Vietnam conflict, the effects of steroid abuse, the Holocaust, survival in the wild, artificial intelligence, World War I battlefields, the sinking of the *Titanic,* the attacks of 9/11, evangelical missionaries in Africa, the Trujillo regime in the Dominican Republic, the assassination of John F. Kennedy, and the French Revolution. In their minds and hearts, they experienced a ballet troupe, juvenile detention facility, Indian reservation, mental ward, inner-city high school, internment camp for Japanese Americans, Soviet-era exile in Siberia, and life for girls growing up in Iran and Afghanistan.

Other teachers whose students read in a workshop can probably identify the novels that Anne's students are referencing. They include Harper Lee's *To Kill a Mockingbird, Life of Pi* by Yann Martel, *Fallen Angels* and *Lockdown* by Walter Dean Myers, *If I Should Die Before I Wake* by Han Nolan, *Crackback* by John Coy, Cynthia Lord's *Rules, Revolution* by Jennifer Donnelly, *Copper Sun* and *Out of My Mind* by Sharon Draper, *The Absolutely True Diary of a Part-Time Indian* by Sherman Alexie, *The Poisonwood Bible* by Barbara Kingsolver, and Deborah Ellis's Breadwinner trilogy.

Just as toddler Anne's vision of the world was enhanced by living inside stories, her adolescent students journey mentally in the company of characters they care for, and,

INSIDE THE READING ZONE

Nolan Conferring With Anne on Memoir

scholastic.com/
RZresources

along the way, develop new frames of reference. The ideas stick because the kids are so affected by the stories: when feelings are stirred, comprehension is assured, and memories are made. The more novels any of us reads, the more memories we make, the richer our vocabularies and networks of knowledge. In several studies that looked at the impact of self-selected reading on knowledge acquisition, participants who did more independent reading consistently scored better on tests of cultural literacy (West and Stanovich, 1991; West, Stanovich, and Mitchell, 1993) *and* practical knowledge *and* science *and* social studies (Stanovich and Cunningham, 1993).

Let me be clear. Testable knowledge is a by-product of reading fiction. It has never been and never will be a primary goal of reading workshop: we do not recommend that teachers select novels for classroom libraries with the aim of improving students' cultural literacy and practical knowledge. The fundamental reason to read fiction is the same as it always has been: the pleasure we feel in the thrall of characters and their stories. But along the way, all sorts of benefits accrue.

In the author's note to his short story collection *Thirteen Ways of Looking*, Colum McCann wrote, "For all its imagined moments, literature works in unimaginable ways" (2015). When the library in their classroom is curated, when it is diverse, literary, and attuned to their interests, young readers get to experience other lives, try on identities, stretch their imaginations, laugh at the ridiculous, weep over the tragic, rage at injustice, travel everywhere, fall in love, appreciate fine writing, recognize when the writing's not so great, and develop fluency, stamina, tastes and preferences, a love of books, and the habit of reading.

This is already enough to ask of novels before factoring in the knowledge bonus, especially in light of research that shows that reading literary fiction makes people more empathetic, which the researchers define as "the capacity to identify and understand others' subjective states" (Kidd and Castano, 2013). Imagining and feeling for characters helps children become less selfish, more thoughtful members of a community.

At the same time, we don't devalue nonfiction or suggest it doesn't belong in reading workshop. A tall bookcase in Anne's classroom is packed with journalism, memoirs, autobiographies, biographies, and books about scientific phenomena. Nonfiction titles popular among her students

> *The more novels any of us reads, the more memories we make, the richer our vocabularies and networks of knowledge.*

> *The fundamental reason to read fiction is the same as it always has been: the pleasure we feel in the thrall of characters and their stories. But along the way, all sorts of benefits accrue.*

include *Into the Wild* and *Into Thin Air* by Jon Krakauer, *A Perfect Storm* by Sebastian Junger, *Unbroken* by Laura Hillenbrand, *Fast Food Nation* by Eric Schlosser, *Persepolis* by Marjane Satrapi, *Maus I* and *Maus II* by Art Spiegelman, *March* and *March 2* by John Lewis and Andrew Aydin, *What If?* by Randall Munroe, David McCullough's *The Wright Brothers*, *Hiroshima* by John Hersey, *I Will Always Write Back* by Caitlin Alifirenka and Martin Ganda, *A Long Way Gone* by Ishmael Beah, Liz Murray's *Breaking Night*, *I Am Malala* by Malala Yousafzai, *The Notorious RBG* by Irin Carmon and Shana Knizhnik, *Being a Beast* by Charles Foster, *But What if We're Wrong?* by Chuck Klosterman, Peter Moore's *The Weather Experiment*, Chelsea Clinton's *It's Your World*, *Zeitoun* by Dave Eggers, and *Beyond Words: What Animals Think and Feel* by Carl Safina.

One common denominator among these fact-based books is that none is a textbook compiled by a committee. Each has a narrative structure and a distinctive voice, as do the books Anne uses to teach American history, the Story of US series by the amazing Joy Hakim (1993–2005). Oscar Wilde wrote, "Books are well written, or badly written. That is all" (1891; 2011). Attributes of good writing cut across genres, and all nonfiction is *not* equal. Informational writing, too, should provide a journey for readers, not presume to fill them up like empty buckets. Readers of every age are meaning makers. Writing that doesn't hold our attention or stir our feelings isn't worthy of intensive study; inevitably, the writing that does takes the form of story.

What's the Story?

Thomas Newkirk posits that people prefer to learn information—and learn it best—from narrative structures. Further, he argues that the line drawn in the Common Core between informational and narrative reading is a false one, because almost everything that's written tells a story. "Narrative is not…merely a type of writing," he observes. "It is a property of mind, an innate and indispensable form of understanding…Good writers know that and construct plots—itches to be scratched—that sustain us as readers. We are always asking, 'What's the story?'" (2014). Or as Gloria Steinem put it, "If you tell me a statistic, I'll make up a story to explain why it's true" (2015).

In reading workshop, Anne leads mini-lessons that invite students to ask, "What's the nonfiction story?" These involve factual topics related to reading, writing, and literature. She eschews commercially prepared text sets of articles previously published in magazines and newspapers as context-stripped exercises. Instead, she reads magazines and newspapers, online as well as in print, and when she finds an article

> " *Narrative is not…merely a type of writing," he observes. "It is a property of mind, an innate and indispensable form of understanding…* "

A fourth-grade reader who loves good true stories gets lost in *A Storm Too Soon* by Michael Touglas

Anne's group discusses recent literary news from *The Guardian* newspaper

that's relevant to her students and their literacy, she photocopies and distributes it and initiates a discussion.

For example, Anne's class read and talked about a feature article from *The New York Times* about series of novels that were supposed to be all wrapped up, except the authors—J. K. Rowling, Maggie Stiefvater, Stephen King—couldn't resist adding one more volume. They read *The Times* full-page obituary for Shakespeare on the 400th anniversary of his death. They read a parody from *The Guardian* of Dan Brown's announcement of a YA version of *The Da Vinci Code*, a feature from *Time* magazine about the blowback following the posthumous publication of Harper Lee's *Go Set a Watchman*, an article from *New York* magazine about the rising popularity of young adult literature among adult readers, and an article from *The New York Times* about how opportunities for quiet reflection and contemplative thinking are being decimated by media devices, not to mention the myth of multitasking. Anne's purpose isn't to satisfy the Common Core by making students practice informational reading. She brings articles to class when she thinks young readers will find them edifying and worth talking about.

In addition to teaching writing and reading, Anne is also responsible for middle school history and current events, and she coaches the school's Model United Nations Team, which includes all of her students. Here, reading serves a different purpose.

Anne wants students to recognize when their goal is to disappear in a story and become lost in it, and when it's to focus on information, ideas, and trying not to become lost. So she teaches them a procedure I developed for how to read and study history and science (see Figure. 8.1), which her students put to use with good effect. And she makes sure, as do her colleagues in grades K–6, that the texts the kids work with are the real thing—trade books, charts and graphs, time lines, primary sources, editorials, position papers, feature articles, and excerpts. Readings that are interesting, worthy, and well written are powerful incentives for students to learn how to look for key concepts and remember them.

How to Read History and Science for Understanding and Retention

1. *Skim* the assigned reading and any illustrations, headings, and sidebars. Create a mental road map of the material, turn on the lights in your brainpan, and activate your long-term memory before you engage as a learner.

2. Choose a writing utensil that's not a highlighter—in other words, one you can write with. Then, as you read a paragraph, underline what seems significant to you.

3. After you finish a paragraph, stop and react to it. Jot a symbol—or two—in the margin.*

    ### SYMBOLS*
    ✓ = I already know this.
    ★ = This is important.
    ? = I have a question, or I'm confused.
    ! = This is surprising or fascinating.
    L = I learned something new.

4. In addition to using the symbols, write a note to yourself in the margin whenever and wherever you can, to push your thinking and create a verbal map you can retrace. Use writing to create thoughts and to make tracks of them.

5. Monitor yourself. Notice when you've become distracted—when you're saying the words without thinking about them, or when your mind has gone off on a little adventure. Bring your brain back to the text, and reread the passage.

6. Read history and science selections twice. Take a short break to let your long-term memory do its thing. The second time through, read the tracks of your thinking, too, plus make any new tracks that occur to you. (Also, consider doing the second reading in a different room in your house: research shows that changing the background improves retention. Go figure.)

7. Now comes the most important part. Put the text aside and engage in an oral retrieval practice. Tell yourself what you remember about the paragraphs you gave stars and Ls to. Ask: What facts, events, names, vocabulary, phenomena, and big ideas can I recall? If you can't answer yourself in-depth, that's a cue to give the material and your tracks another skim or reread, especially your stars and Ls. Then test yourself again.

QUESTION: How can you take advantage of this study procedure in high school classes where you're not allowed to write in the book?

ANSWER: That's why God made those teeny tiny sticky notes.

* Adapted from Harvey and Daniels (2009).

FIGURE 8.1 How to Read History and Science for Understanding and Retention

Anne assigns readings about history only in history class, never in reading workshop. Like me, she believes content integration hurts the teaching of reading and literature. We notice that no one expects math teachers to integrate history and science into their lessons—the integrity of math instruction is a given. English teachers need to stand up for the integrity of our own subjects. It's a monumental task—and obligation—to introduce and nurture what matters about literature, reading, and the craft and conventions of writing. Our students can't afford for us to surrender a single one of our precious 180 days to the teaching of history and science.

Ursula K. Le Guin wrote, "There have been great societies that did not use the wheel, but there have been no societies that did not tell stories" (1970). Facts—and wheels—matter, a lot. But narrative "is the vehicle of culture, understanding, interpretation, and supporting detail...it is the *artful narrative about the facts* that gives them meaning" (Kirby, 2016).

The Power and Pleasure of Story

Flash back with me to 1990. It's a sunny morning in our kitchen on the island. Anne climbs aboard the foot I'm swinging and asks for a ride. "Come on," she coaxes. "We're going on a boat to America. Far across the water." She doesn't have the word yet, but thanks to *Watch the Stars Come Out*, an artful narrative by Riki Levinson, she has the concept. Because fiction is helping to shape her essence, immigration has become part of her experience.

Engaging with literature enables children to know things, feel things, imagine things, hope for things, *become people* they—and we—couldn't have dreamed of otherwise because of the transforming power and ultimate pleasure of story.

CHAPTER NINE

High School by Anne

An eighth grader booktalks his beloved *The Great Gatsby*

After CTL, our students head off in different directions to all kinds of secondary schools, where they shine. Many go on to the public high schools in their towns; some enroll at private day schools in Maine; others attend parochial schools; a few matriculate at northeastern boarding schools. While their post-CTL destinations vary, their experience of high school English and their feelings about it are, by and large, the same. Reading as they've known it—passionately, voluminously, according to their own tastes and preferences, with original ideas and analyses in response—no longer exists for them.

I checked in with a cross-section of our graduates, students who attend each type of secondary school. Despite their excitement about their flourishing social lives and stellar grades, our conversations were discouraging. All of them considered themselves "less of a reader" than they were during their CTL years. In fact, every one of them qualified their response: "*Much* less."

Research suggests they are not alone. A meta-analysis by Common Sense Media (2014) shows that almost half of U.S. 17-year-olds report reading for pleasure *no more than once or twice a year*. This has serious repercussions for their academic success: another study, by the National Center for Education Statistics (2011), found that high schoolers who read in their leisure time score significantly higher on measures of reading ability.

When I talked in depth with CTL graduates, the reasons for their diminished identities as readers became clear. The biggest change in these once-voracious consumers of fiction and nonfiction is that they don't read very much, for school or at home. They cite the small number of books they're assigned to read by their English teachers and the time-consuming quizzes, discussions, written paragraphs, group assignments, projects, and essays they have to do in response. The activities replace actual reading. Sophomore Lydia noted that most of the assignments feel like assessments "done for the kids who don't read. And people in my high school really don't like reading."

Inching Their Way Through Just a Few Books

Most of the alums read only three to five books during an entire year of high school. These are the same students who read 30, 40, 50, even 100 or more books between September and June as seventh and eighth graders. These are the same students I described in final reports—and who described themselves in self-evaluations—as "passionate," "voracious," "literary," "lifelong" readers. These are the same students who begged to give booktalks, eagerly awaited the next round of letter-essays, and tried to pry new titles from my hands as soon as they appeared in the classroom.

Now they're inching their way through three to five books a year. Zachary, a junior, characterized the snail-like pace of his English class as "*very* slow, to make sure we hit on every metaphor or simile." He referenced "Introduction to Poetry," a Billy Collins poem we had discussed in reading workshop, in which Collins despairs at the practice of "beating [a poem] with a hose/to find out what it really means" (1996). Zachary said, "A lot of times we're going into minutiae that isn't necessary to understand the book… it's a slog."

Kids who know what it is to get lost between book covers told me how inauthentic this pace feels. Lydia explained, "It's hard to get into a book because we have to make so many notes along the way. I actually tend not to do what the teacher says—I read the book straight through without interruptions, so it sinks in better, and then I go back and make the notes." Ryan is similarly frustrated: "I like to read at my own pace. What's crazy about how slowly we go through the books is that you don't even really have to read them—it's all gone over in class anyway."

Ryan isn't the only alum who perceives this approach as spoonfeeding, rather than demonstrating the "rigor" his private school's website advertises. Amelia, author of the *Scarlet Pimpernel* letter-essay in Chapter 6, drew an insightful distinction. "CTL was *truly* rigorous," she said. "This past year we only read five books. Analysis is more based on surface-level picking apart of syntax and diction. It's a lot less in-depth. And we don't talk about theme in the same way or come up with original ideas about the reading."

Penny Kittle has written about the difficulty that high school students face—and the disservice high school teachers do them—when they move from four years of reading very little to their freshman year of college, where expectations for reading within a single week can be anywhere between 200 and 600 pages (2013). Ironically, when I had taught the alums as seventh- and eighth-grade readers, they were probably better prepared for the freshman year of college than their freshman year of high school.

Why do my former students think they read so much less now? It comes down to a lack of what reading workshop provides: choice of books, invitations to intriguing titles, time to read, and a culture of peers and teachers who prioritize book reading.

Most of the alums entered schools where, as Ryan remarked, "There is absolutely no choice built into the curriculum." Their lack of say in the books they read is identified as *the* key difference between middle school and their reading lives—or lack thereof—in high school. They recognize that choice is what made them love reading, and they miss the opportunity to select titles that engage them.

> *Their lack of say in the books they read is identified as the key difference between middle school and their reading lives—or lack thereof—in high school. They recognize that choice is what made them love reading, and they miss the opportunity to select titles that engage them.*

The Indispensable Support of a Reading Community

A couple of the alums attend a school that does assign outside, free-choice books, but, as one explained, "It's just an afterthought, compared with the assigned reading and writing." It is also an assignment with no teacher support. Without introductions to good books, without classroom libraries, kids have no idea what books to choose. Zachary found himself going back to his middle school Someday List and tracking down novels by Kurt Vonnegut, along with the kinds of memoirs and journalism he'd loved at CTL: *This Boy's Life* by Tobias Wolff and Hunter S. Thompson's *Fear and Loathing in Las Vegas*. He also said he notices that his peers don't know their own reading preferences, that they seem to select blindly among bestselling page-turners. He found himself becoming a book resource for his friends, who do respond to his guidance. "The reading community is there," he said, "but it's not obvious."

Without a supportive, informed reading community, the high schoolers had stopped growing as readers. Every graduate of CTL leaves with strong preferences, one hallmark of a true reader. Off the tops of their heads and with great enthusiasm, they can and do cite their favorite authors and poets. By contrast, only one of the alums I checked in with was able to name a new favorite author or poet encountered via a high school reading assignment. Most referred back to preferences they had formed in middle school. The best anyone could do was name an assigned novel they had liked—Amelia loved *Crime and Punishment*, for example. But as Sara noted, "We don't really read enough to figure out what authors we might like." Lydia concurred: "It's hard now to get an idea of different poets' styles because we might, maybe, read one poem by one poet. And it's hard to explore different authors, because I don't have time to look into books by writers I might like."

Scarcity of time came up in every single interview. Of course, teenagers are busy—with homework, sports, clubs, jobs, and family commitments. CTL's alums aren't alone in this. In a Bureau of Labor Statistics report on how Americans spend their leisure time, 15- to 19-year-olds spend fewer minutes reading than any other age group (2015). Zachary shed a bit of light on why this would be. "It's not the same when reading isn't part of your schoolwork or homework. Because independent reading is *not* something teachers consider when assigning homework, it's much more difficult to find the time to read."

What Happens in Class?

What are my former students doing during all this class time that doesn't involve actual reading? They described long weeks spent in small groups devoted to particular aspects of a novel—the imagery group in this corner; the historical context group in that corner; report out every Friday. They told me about frequent long tests with "vocab sections, passage ID sections, and literary device sections." They talked about having to write a new chapter from the main character's perspective. They talked about an entire month of class time spent listening to classmates painstakingly read *Romeo and Juliet*. They talked about more small group work, this time devoted to completing a handout for every chapter of the class novel. They talked about in-class essays. They talked about SAT test prep—being handed a passage they'd never seen before to read, write about, and get graded on, with no opportunity for feedback or discussion. They are experiencing what Kelly Gallagher calls "constant over-teaching, constant teacher-induced interruptions, the constant chopping up of great books" (2009). And they are barely reading.

In the first edition of this book, Nancie fleshed out an analogy I find useful in thinking about the travesty of the one-chapter-at-a-time approach to whole-class novels.

> Imagine the impact on us if this were our history with another narrative artform, the movies. Instead of disappearing into the black cocoon of a theater, living inside a film, letting the experience of it settle inside us, and then formulating a response to the vision of its writer and director, what if we had to anticipate the approach of an authority figure who, every fifteen minutes, turned off the projector, threw on the houselights, gave us a quiz, and called on us to participate in a discussion of the movie-so-far? I don't think many of us would come to appreciate the emotional and intellectual power of a great visual story. I do think the effect of reading and talking about a novel in bits and pieces is similar (2007).

Again, although the kids I talked with attend a variety of kinds of secondary schools, their literary experiences are largely the same. I wasn't surprised. They were describing *my* high school reading years.

My History as a Reader

The time I spent in high school was the Dark Ages of an otherwise vibrant, fulfilling, stimulating childhood with books. At home and in my K–8 years at CTL, I lived and breathed books. My parents read to me until the language of favorite titles became engraved in my memory, until the words became my own. *A Time of Wonder*, Robert McCloskey's prose poem about summer on a Maine island, was real to me before I had a reality of my own. Under the influence of McCloskey I explored shells on the beach, listened for the birdsong that signaled early morning, sang at the top of my lungs during a storm, and recognized that a time would come when I would have to leave my island.

As a girl without a sense yet of what being female might mean, I read Alcott's *Little Women*, Austen's *Pride and Prejudice,* and the Anne of Green Gables series by L. M. Montgomery, and I learned that I wanted to be an outspoken, opinionated girl, too. Jo, Elizabeth, and Anne taught me the beauty of dreams, but also how to be strong and never constrained by gender—how to hold my own against a Laurie, a Mr. Darcy, a Gilbert Blythe. When I returned to my own world, I had new ideas about the woman I wanted to become.

My reading shaped my identity; it flooded me with vicarious experiences, helped form the questions I thought were worth asking, and provided a prism through which I viewed the world and imagined my place in it.

Then came high school. The first sign of trouble came fall of freshman year, after I turned in the summer reading assignment. I'd painstakingly completed a double-entry log, writing paragraph-length analyses of what I determined to be the significant passages from the assigned book. I was mortified to see the low grade that adorned my log when the teacher returned it. Since she had written no comments, I asked a friend who'd done well if I could read her log, to figure out what I'd missed. Her pages were filled with quotes—many more than I had chosen—each with a single-sentence "connection" inscribed beside it along the lines of "I can relate to this because my sister and I fight, too." This teacher was looking for lots of personal cross-references, not the literary analysis I had produced. *Okay, I can do this*, I thought. *And I will. But it's pointless. And I'm going to hate it.*

My classmates and I inched our way through *The Canterbury Tales* and *The Catcher in the Rye*, reading from class sets of the books in 15-page increments and then taking weeks to create small-group posters about

> *My reading shaped my identity; it flooded me with vicarious experiences, helped form the questions I thought were worth asking, and provided a prism through which I viewed the world and imagined my place in it.*

one of Chaucer's characters, or losing points on a quiz for failing to remember the color of Holden Caulfield's scarf. Even stories I *knew* I loved lost their sense of magic. This wasn't the *Hamlet* that had brought me to tears when I saw it performed onstage with my parents or watched Kenneth Branagh breathe life into it in my seventh-grade drama class. This couldn't be *The Great Gatsby,* one of my favorite books in eighth grade, when it had meant so much more to me than a crib note that read "Green light = envy, money."

I was lucky to have parents who are English teachers of another stripe to help me put all this into perspective. My mom continued to booktalk titles to me so that my Someday List, now a mental one, remained full, and I continued to be intrigued by stories whenever I could squeeze a space for them. Books became something separate from my academic experience; they became a lifeline. Despite staying up late doing homework, I set my alarm a half-hour early each morning—no easy feat for a teenager—so I could spend time in the worlds created by Margaret Atwood, Barbara Kingsolver, and Michael Ondaatje. School vacations were the only time when I could unstack the tower of books on my bedside table and spend hours, if not days, lost in the zone. My summer job was so much better than school because I got a half-hour lunch break during which I could read—*The Amazing Adventures of Kavalier and Clay* by Michael Chabon or A. S. Byatt's *Possession.*

I compartmentalized. I divided my love of reading and my dread of English class into different realms: my escape from and lens for viewing the world vs. the drudgery of in-class oral reading and sticky notes. I also reasoned that my middle-school love of reading had been a fluke. I no longer liked the school subject I had thought was my favorite. Maybe reading would always be a hobby, but I was eager to reach the end of this thing called English class.

College was an epiphany. After a freshman year spent avoiding anything labeled ENGL in the course catalog, one day I found myself ordering texts at the bookstore. While I picked up the materials for my history and psychology classes, my eyes wandered to the shelves where the English course materials were stacked. Virginia Woolf winked at me. Tolstoy beckoned. Toni Morrison smiled enigmatically.

One English course turned into a major. I couldn't get enough. I loved the way we were assigned a week to read a book independently and then talked about the whole thing as a complete work of literature. We debated themes and characters and authors' styles and techniques. We wrote papers for which we developed our own theses. My professors had pulled together syllabi that excited *them*, full of authors and works they loved, and their enthusiasm for literature was as contagious as that of my old CTL teachers giving booktalks and leading poetry discussions. I was home; I was back in the zone.

As an English teacher who teaches writing and reading in a workshop, I can't imagine a more rewarding vocation. Because I experienced the reading zone and then the loss of it, I am determined to create and maintain it for my students. My own experience also taught me that, once a reader has found it, the zone never truly goes away.

I tell the alums this. My former CTL peers confirm it to a one: they also came back to reading after the desert of high school. Today they read the most, the most consistently, and with the most pleasure of any grown-ups I know.

> *…memories of the zone can sustain us…But why create obstacles to the reading life, especially during years critical to academic, social, and emotional growth and personal identity?*

Imagining a High School Reading Zone

It seems that memories of the zone can sustain us, given the odds stacked against them by high school English teachers and curricula. But why create obstacles to the reading life, especially during years critical to academic, social, and emotional growth and personal identity?

I know that my professional colleagues who teach high school English entered the field because of their own love of literature, and that many confront institutional hurdles to instilling book love in their students—tradition, department guidelines, and standards, most recently those of the Common Core. But these systems are not working for kids, aren't creating the kinds of readers I think we can all agree we would like them to become.

I asked my former students *how could it be different?* What would you change about high school English? Their responses returned to common themes: time, choice, introductions to good books, authentic assignments, and a reading culture. The follow-up question becomes *how?* Nancie pondered this question in the first edition of *The Reading Zone*:

This eighth grader will leave CTL with a passion for books by Dave Eggers

How does such a process get started? I think it begins when high school English teachers step outside the curriculum and think—and talk—about who they want students to be when they graduate: What kinds of readers? What kinds of writers? What would your goals be for your students if you were to think of them as if they were your own children, and then dream for them as a *literary parent* might?

I think I know the answer. Teachers would want every high school graduate to be able to read fluently, deeply, and with pleasure. The logical follow-up is *how?* Well, perhaps by trying to ease the way for students to read a lot and love books. And maybe by putting frequent, sustained, pleasurable experiences with books at the heart—or at least as an essential part—of the secondary curriculum (2007).

My own first suggestion is to offer kids choice. It *is* valuable for kids to engage with a shared text, analyzing it with the support of an expert, experienced reader. In my middle-school classroom, this takes the form of the poetry discussions described in Chapter 7. Richard Allington and Penny Kittle have found success using shared texts with high school students between 20 and 30 percent of the time, while Kelly Gallagher outlines how he divides a school year to include opportunities for both independent reading and whole-class or "core" works, which allow his students to read, discuss, and respond to many more works of literature than the typical high school English timetable permits (2015).

Multiple studies have found that allowing students to choose their own books results in more involvement in reading and greater overall motivation (Sewell, 2003; Gallagher, 2009; Pruzinsky, 2014). And choice of books lets high schoolers do the most important, challenging work of adolescence—figuring out who they are and who they want to become. We are doing teenagers a disservice if we don't allow them this opportunity, as Nancie puts it, to try to make sense of adulthood.

> *And choice of books lets high schoolers do the most important, challenging work of adolescence—figuring out who they are and who they want to become.*

My second suggestion concerns volume. High school kids need to be reading *more*. Multiple studies show that the amount of independent reading kids do correlates significantly with reading achievement (Swan et al., 2010; Hiebert & Reutzel, 2010; Cunningham & Stanovich, 2003). The Common Core State Standards set no targets for how much students will read. Worse, they implicitly encourage a movement away from quantity by emphasizing the use of excerpts and informational text, which hardly provide the volume of sustained reading experiences that literature does. And we know that voluminous, sustained reading experiences are vitally important to the development of reading ability.

Next, students will need ideas and inspiration for titles worthy of independent reading—as Nancie put it, their teachers "need to *expect and help* high school students to read a lot." Research by John Guthrie and Nicole Humenick found that access to a variety of intriguing and enjoyable books has a profound effect on both reading comprehension and motivation to read (2004). I encourage English teachers to work with school librarians to make up-to-date collections of excellent young adult and adult transitional titles accessible to their students—to give booktalks about titles they've read or read reviews of, consult *VOYA* magazine, invite the librarian into the classroom to booktalk new releases, and build a classroom library or a display of borrowed library books, their covers facing enticingly forward. Kelly Gallagher begins each class with a Reading Minute, a brief endorsement of a book. He keeps a Books We Recommend Binder and regularly places individual titles on each desk in his classroom and invites students to do a book pass, where they're able to page through and preview many volumes in pursuit of their next read (2015).

These are all important steps in creating a culture of reading in high school. Social needs drive adolescents, and a shared reading culture is key to my middle school students' engagement with books. They eagerly pass books back and forth, trade theories about plot points, and monitor the titles their friends are enjoying as they make plans for what to read next. None of this is happening in high school. In explaining why she had read zero books beyond the three assigned titles during her junior year, Sara said, "The motivation to read on my own isn't there. It's hard to go back when it's not surrounding me. The social structure for being a reader doesn't exist here."

An eighth-grade reader who already has teenage style

Lydia summed up her current feeling—and frustration—about reading: "It just can't be on the top of my list anymore. I wish I could go back and have that time again and have it be that important to the people around me, especially my teachers." Teachers need to make reading a priority in their classes so students will receive the message that it's important. Elementary grade children and beginning readers get this message constantly—and read more and more often as a result. Teenagers need to receive the message too.

The only sure way to convince kids that reading has high-priority status is to give them time to read in class. When teachers integrate time for reading workshop into the schedule, it becomes part of the fabric of a student's academic experience. It is worth it. Research shows that kids who read for pleasure demonstrate more growth in their vocabulary *and* their spelling *and* their math skills than peers who rarely read (Sullivan and Brown, 2013). I encourage high school English departments to address two questions that Nancie poses: "What's the best use of the brief time we've got with them?" and "What do we let go of, so we can focus on students becoming skilled, passionate, habitual, critical readers?" (2007).

The Intellectual Life Around Them

The Russian psycholinguist L. S. Vygotsky wrote, "Children grow into the intellectual life around them" (1978). When the alums I spoke with were in middle school, the intellectual environment was rich: full of books, lively discussions, and passionate readers. In high school, a time in their lives when they want to become the authors of their own identities, find their place in a community, and search for meaning in the larger world, the intellectual life that students encounter should be *even more* stimulating. Imagine the people who would enter adulthood after four years of books that engage and intrigue them, peers who are passionate about reading, and teachers who find the right volumes to put in their hands and then give them time to read them. These are scholars and citizens we would be honored to know and proud to have taught.

CHAPTER TEN

Practicalities

Effective teachers of any subject develop a habit of finding and solving problems. Over decades of teaching reading as a workshop, I found lots of practical problems; I was still experimenting with solutions when I retired from the classroom. Now Anne and her K–6 colleagues continue the tradition. These are CTL's current best ideas when it comes to the nitty-gritty details of maintaining a healthy reading zone.

Author baskets make life easier for grades 1–2 readers

Time

Every teacher whom Anne and I know feels constrained by time. Even at CTL, where teachers determine the schedule, we wrestle with what's possible to accommodate in a seven-and-a-half-hour school day. We think and talk, often and always, about *priorities*. There has to be a snack break midmorning, so children can ingest some fresh calories to burn, and a healthy noon recess, weather permitting, outside on the playground and field or otherwise in the gym. Kids need chunks of time for art, music or drama, and phys. ed. at least once a week, plus science and history at least three times a week, writing workshop at least four days a week, and math class and reading workshop every day.

The baseline schedule for our K–8 school and our shared teaching spaces is included in my book *Systems to Transform Your Classroom and School* (2014), along with descriptions of our policies and traditions, methods and resources, assessment and teaching innovations, and expectations and guidelines for reading—and writing—workshop at multiple grade levels.

In the seventh and eighth grades, time gets tighter because we departmentalize and add a science teacher and a math teacher. So Anne combines writing and reading in an 85-minute language arts block and breaks the block into five segments.

Writing-Reading Workshop

- **Daily poem:** 10 minutes
- **Writing or reading mini-lesson:** 5–15 minutes *(Atwell, 2002; 2015)*
- **Independent writing and individual conferring:** 30 minutes
- **Booktalks or a read-aloud from the genre kids are studying in writing:** 10 minutes
- **Independent reading and individual conferring:** 20 minutes

On Tuesdays and Thursdays, Anne's students, as well as those in grades 3–6 writing workshops, take about five minutes for individualized spelling studies (Atwell, 2015).

Dividing the block of time this way accomplishes three things. It fits with what educators know about the attention spans of young adolescents and how it aids their learning when they can shift among activities. It's predictable: students anticipate and make plans for their engagement with particular books and particular pieces of writing. And it cuts to the chase by concentrating on what matters most in an English class, and that is the authentic work of writers, readers, and critics.

In my previous teaching position, I taught students twice a day: one 50-minute period for English, which I established as a writing workshop, and a second for reading, which became reading workshop. It was wonderful. While I recognize that more middle and high schools are turning to block schedules, the single 50-minute period is still the norm. If this were my teaching assignment, I'd get together with the colleagues who teach my kids and try to arrange a block schedule among us, for example, trade off single-period classes with the math teacher and create double periods twice a week for math class and writing-reading workshop.

Kindergarteners and Caroline in CTL's Primary Reading Room for their daily workshop

If there were simply no way to shake extended chunks of time out of the system, I'd still establish a predictable, bedrock schedule, one students could count on and plan for: three days of writing workshop, two days of reading workshop, and, for homework seven nights a week, half an hour of pleasure reading. I'd allocate more class time to writing because kids have to write at least three days a week if they're going to demonstrate growth as writers (Graves, 1983) and because they need more teacher support for their writing. Students can read at home more productively than they can write at home.

I'd teach a writing mini-lesson on the three days students are writing. On reading workshop days, I'd plan mini-lessons related to books, authors, or reading, as well as a booktalk or three, and monitor students' at-home reading by multiplying by 20 the number of days since I'd last checked in about where each is in his or her book. In other words, if the most recent reading workshop were on a Monday, kids should be at least 80 pages further along at the start of reading workshop on Friday.

Guidelines and Expectations

Whatever the schedule—language arts block or single-period English—the goals for reading workshop are the same: it's a time and a place for students to behave as passionate, habitual, critical readers. In September, Anne explains her expectations for reading workshop: in a nutshell, what middle school kids have to do in order to become skilled, passionate, habitual, critical readers. The expectations that CTL teachers of grades 1–6 communicate to their students are adapted from these.

Whatever the schedule—language arts block or single-period English—the goals for reading workshop are the same: it's a time and a place for students to behave as passionate, habitual, critical readers.

Ted's group in CTL's Reading Room for their first-thing-in-the-morning reading workshop

Glenn's group takes over the CTL Reading Room in the midmorning block between snack recess and lunchtime

Jill's third and fourth graders get lost in the zone in the Reading Room during the afternoon block at CTL

Expectations for Reading This Year

· Read as much as you can, as joyfully as you can. Practice with pleasure.

· Read at home for at least half an hour every day, seven days a week.

· Find books, authors, subjects, genres, and themes that matter to who you are now, who you once were, and who you might become.

· Try new books, authors, subjects, genres, and themes. Expand your literary experience, knowledge, and appreciation.

· On the Someday List in your writing-reading handbook (Atwell, 2015), keep a running list of titles and authors you'd like to try, especially in response to booktalks and other recommendations.

· Recognize that a book represents a writer's ideas and the choices he or she made. Understand that you can step back from a story after you've finished living inside it and notice and discuss the author's decisions.

· Use the critical vocabulary you already know and the terms I teach you to talk and write about literature.

· Write a letter-essay every three weeks about what you noticed and appreciated about one book you've recently finished. Use writing to go back inside the book as a critic and consider the writing—how the book made you think and feel, what the author did, what worked or needs more work.

· Recognize that there are different approaches to reading and different stances readers take in relation to different texts, e.g., realistic fiction vs. a poem vs. a feature article in a newspaper vs. a chapter from a history book vs. a scientific report.

· Develop and articulate your own criteria for selecting and abandoning books.

· Each trimester, establish and work toward significant, relevant goals for yourself as a reader.

· In every reading workshop take a *deliberate stance* (Harwayne, 1992) toward engaging and responding with your whole heart and mind. Take advantage of the workshop—*use it* to find your own sources of happiness and inspiration. Stretch your imagination, live other lives and learn about your own, find prose and poetry so well written it knocks you out, understand experiences you might never know about otherwise, find stories that make you happy and feed your soul, consider how other writers have written and why, acquire their knowledge and insights, wonder, escape, think, travel, ponder, laugh, cry, love, and grow up.

Throughout the rest of the school year, Anne organizes her teaching so kids can make good on her expectations. The conditions for engaged reading that students identified in Chapter 2 function as a set of expectations for the teacher: what kids can count on from Anne so they'll be able to immerse in the zone.

Whether students read in class for two days a week or five, teachers need to establish and stick with basic rules that promote engagement and combat distraction during independent reading time. Ten guidelines direct CTL readers of grades 3–8 into the reading zone.

Rules for Reading Workshop

1. You must read a book. Magazines, newspapers, and comics don't offer the extended chunks of prose you need to develop fluency. More important, they won't help you discover who you are as a reader of books.

2. Don't read a book you don't like. Don't waste time with a book you don't love when there are so many great ones waiting for you—*unless* you decide to finish a bad book so you can criticize it. Do develop your own system for abandoning books.

3. If you don't like your book, find another. Check out the Books-We-Love display. Check your list of Someday books. Browse our shelves. Ask me or a friend for a recommendation.

4. It's more than all right to reread a book you love. This is something good readers do.

5. It's okay to skim or skip parts of a book if you get bored or stuck. Good readers do this, too.

6. On the form inside your reading folder, record the title of every book you finish or abandon, its genre and author and difficulty level (Holiday, Just Right, or Challenge), the date, and your rating, 1–10. Collect data about yourself as a reader, look for patterns, and take satisfaction in your accomplishments.

7. Understand that reading is thinking. Do nothing that distracts your classmates from the reading zone: don't put your words into their brains as they're trying to escape into the worlds of words that authors create. When you talk to me about your book, use as soft a voice as I use when I talk with you. *Whisper.*

8. Take care of our books. Sign out every one you borrow on your card set, and then sign it back in *with me*—I'll draw a line through the title and initial the card. Return the book to its section in our library, alphabetically by the author's last name, or, if it's a book you loved, add it to the Books-We-Love collection.

9. Read the whole time.

10. Read as much as you can.

Student record-keeping is essentially the same in grades K–8. Every child has a reading folder that stays in the classroom, stored in a crate or file drawer. Inside each folder the teacher fastens multiple copies of a form on which students record the title of each book, its author and genre, the date they finished or abandoned it, an overall rating of 1–10, and whether it was a Holiday (H), Just Right (JR), or Challenge (C). To help older readers determine the more specific genres their books represent, Figure 10.1 is a master list of genres that's kept up to date by Anne's students. Kids in grades 5–8 keep copies of it in a pocket of their reading folders for easy reference.

Genres . . . So Far

- action-adventure
- alternative history
- antiwar novel
- autobiography
- biography
- classic
- comic novel
- contemporary realistic fiction
- diary
- dystopian science fiction
- epic poem
- epistolary novel
- essay anthology or collection
- family saga

- fantasy
- flash-fiction anthology or collection
- free-verse memoir or novel
- gothic novel
- graphic history, journalism, or memoir
- graphic novel
- historical fiction
- history
- horror
- humorous essays
- instructional guide
- journalism

- law novel
- legend
- magical realism
- manga
- memoir
- mystery: plot or psychological
- mythology
- new journalism
- paranormal fiction
- parody
- philosophy
- play script
- poetry anthology or collection
- post-apocalyptic sci fi
- punk fairy tale

- retelling/recasting
- romance
- science
- science fiction
- series novel
- short story anthology or collection
- sports novel
- spy novel
- steam punk novel
- supernatural
- techno-thriller
- thriller
- Western

FIGURE 10.1 Genres…So Far

Reading Record for <u>Luke Gr. 7</u>

Nancie Atwell
Center for Teaching and Learning

#	TITLE	GENRE	AUTHOR	DATE FINISHED	DATE ABANDONED	RATING	LEVEL
1	The Martian	Sci-Fi	Andy Weir	9-21-15	—	10	JR
2	Michael Vey #5	Act. Ad	Richard Paul Evans	9-26	—	8	JR
3	Death Cure	Dystopia	James Dashner	10-3	~	9	JR
4	Kill order	Dystopia	James Dashner	10-10	—	10	JR
5	Monument 14	Dystopia	Emmy Laybourne	10-16	—	9	JR
6	Zeitoun	non-fiction	Dave Eggers	10-24	—	10	CH
7	Code Talker	non-fiction	Chester Nez	10-30	—	10	CH.
8	Every Day	Magical realism	David Levithan	11-6	—	10	JR
9	The Rig	Action	Joe Ducie	11-14	-	9	JR
10	5th Wave	dystopia	Rick Yancey	11-22	—	10	JR
11	Legend	dystopian Sci-Fi	Marie Lu	11-30	—	10	JR
12	Prodigy	dystopian Sci-Fi	Marie Lu	12-7	—	9	JR
13	Worst Class Trip Ever	Humor	Dave Barry	12-14	—	10	H
14	Rage Within	Disaster	Jeyn Roberts	12-21	—	10	JR
15	Red Queen	Dystopia	Victoria Aveyard	1-5	—	9	JR
16	Game	sports fiction	Walter Myers	1-10	~	10	JR
17	Gone	dystopia	Michael Grant	1-17	~	10	JR
18	Jurassic Park	dystopia	Michael Crichton	1-20	~	9	JR
19	The Lost World	Dystopia	Michael Crichton	1-23	~	10	JR
20	Boy 21	sports fiction	Matthew Quick	1-26	~	10	JR
21	Fate of Ten	Dystopia	Pittacus Lore	2-3	—	10	JR
22	All-American Boys	CRF	Jason Reynolds + Brendan Kiely	2-9	—	9	JR
23	Illuminae	dystopia	Amie Kaufman	3-14	—	10	JR
24	I Hunt Killers	horror	Barry Lyga	2-21	~	10	JR

FIGURE 10.2 The first page of a seventh-grade boy's reading record

Students' reading records are useful to them, their teachers, and their parents as regular snapshots of a child's progress, habits, and preferences. And when it comes time for formal assessment at the end of a trimester, reading records provide essential data.

Assessment

When they read in a workshop, students are in a constant state of evaluation. They collect data, select and reject, assess what is and isn't working in the books and poems they read, form judgments, give ratings, present booktalks, make plans, notice pace, monitor productivity, recognize when they need help, and ask for it. So formal assessment at CTL begins with self-evaluation, with the child's analysis of his or her work as a reader. We stop the workshop for a week so kids have time both to look back—to notice and reflect on accomplishments and progress— and to look ahead to what they need or want to do next. The process starts with a self-evaluation questionnaire. Children write—or, in K–1, dictate—answers to questions about their preferences, literary criteria, accomplishments, progress, and goals.

> *…formal assessment at CTL begins with self-evaluation, with the child's analysis of his or her work as a reader.*

Seventh and eighth graders and Anne in their reading workshop in the CTL Humanities Room

Basic Questions for Self-Assessment in Reading

- How many books did you finish this trimester?

- How many were Holidays, Just Rights, or Challenges?

- What genres are represented?

- Which book of the trimester was the best one? Why: what did the author do in crafting it?

- Which three poems of the trimester were the best ones? Why: what did the poets do in crafting them?

- What were your breakthroughs and accomplishments as a reader this trimester? Consider your pace, productivity, risks and challenges, new authors and genres, responses in discussions, booktalks, changes in your letter-essays, how you choose books, how you make and use plans, etc.

- What are your favorite genres to read these days?

- Who are your favorite authors these days? Why these writers?

- Who are your favorite poets? Why these poets?

- What was your favorite read-aloud? Why?

- What progress did you make toward each of the goals we set at the end of last trimester?

- What are your goals for yourself as a reader next trimester in terms of:

    your productivity and pace: number of books or of pages per night?

    your book choices?

    your experiments with genres and authors?

    your written responses to books in letter-essays?

    your booktalks?

    your participation in poetry discussions?

Depending on the focus of mini-lessons in a given trimester, we've also included questions that ask readers to consider:

- What was your favorite memoir/flash fiction/essay read-aloud? Why? What did the author do in crafting it?

- What are the most important things you're able to do as a critic of and responder to prose: what can you notice, react to, and express?

- What's a book that took you by surprise this trimester? Why?

- What will you take away from our study of the poetry of William Carlos Williams?

- What are the most important implications for you of our study of reading as a psycholinguistic process?

- How are the letter-essays working for you as a critic?

- What's something new you tried as a reader in terms of author, genre, or process? How did it work for you?

- In your experience so far as a reader and writer of poems, what are the most significant things poetry does for you as a person?

- Please finish this sentence as many ways as you can: *I realize the following things about myself as a reader:*

In June, at the end of the third trimester, Anne asks students to retake an adapted version of the September reading survey, and then she returns the originals to them. Her kids use this as one form of information when all the children at CTL research and write about their growth in summative self-assessments, which teachers file in students' permanent records. These are voiced, interesting, accurate, often moving accounts of kids' perceptions of who they are as readers and critics.

Every student at our school compiles a portfolio each year: a three-ring binder filled with representative, captioned examples of work across the disciplines. Then, informed by the children's self-assessments and portfolios, teachers write comments about each student's progress, accomplishments, strengths, and challenges in every subject area and create a final list of individual goals: a combination of those the student generated and any others the teacher deems essential.

The student, teacher, and parents meet in an evaluation conference led by the child, in which he or she presents the portfolio, and the teacher shares comments and goals. If a grade is being assigned, it's based on the progress a student made toward accomplishing the goals that were set at the end of the previous trimester. Chapters in *Systems* (2014) and in *In the Middle* (2015) are devoted to the minutiae of valuing and evaluating reading and setting goals and grades.

Simone: A Case Study

It may be illuminating to look at one student—Simone, a seventh grader new to CTL—and see how the assessment process nurtured her growth. When Simone entered CTL, she did not consider herself a reader. "It's so boring," was the frequent refrain. When Anne described the standard expectation of 30 minutes of nightly reading, Simone despaired. "I'd just rather be doing something else. Anything else."

She and Anne talked about her reading in daily check-ins, with Anne asking her what she was responding to positively and what she disliked. At first Simone wanted only to read and reread the Twilight series by Stephenie Meyer. She abandoned almost every book that didn't suck her in on its first page. In the first trimester, she reluctantly read eight books, most of them by Meyer.

Simone's goals for the second trimester were to make sure she read *at least* 30 minutes every single night, to abandon only one book, to pay attention to peers' booktalks, and to experiment with titles and authors that corresponded to her personal interests—contemporary realism with strong, emotionally complex female protagonists and books that resonated with her love of animals. She and Anne stapled her list of goals to the front pocket of her reading folder, after discussing them with her mother during their parent-teacher-student conference.

And Simone began to enter the reading zone. Intriguing plots, like that of E. Lockhart's *We Were Liars*, began to catch and hold her attention. She discovered she enjoyed books by the young adult novelists Gayle Forman, Jenny Han, and Rainbow Rowell, as well as the memoir *Alex and Me*, Irene Pepperberg's story of her bond with an African grey parrot and the insights she gleaned into animal intelligence. Simone's new friends in the class began making recommendations, too, not just in booktalks. The girls gossiped about the novels and their characters as if they were acquaintances and drew up informal waiting lists for in-demand titles.

In seventh grade, Simone read 30 books and in eighth grade 44. Her favorite authors that year were Stephen King, Marcus Zusak, and Agatha Christie. Her favorite poets were Wallace Stevens and Langston Hughes. She loved historical fiction now but continued to adore nonfiction books about animal behavior. And she had an identity as a reader. She wrote: "I'm a fast reader who's great at choosing books I'll like. I'm really good at drawing out the theme in any book." Here, and in her graduation speech, she proclaimed, "I love to read."

The assessment process helped both of us take a long view on what was happening with Simone as a reader—basically an unwillingness to engage the muscles of her imagination when it came to trying and committing to unfamiliar stories and characters. A combination of personalized expectations that pushed her and personalized advice that helped her meet the expectations made it possible for Simone to be brave, to immerse in a new crop of books that she loved, and to become a reader. Tom Romano observed, "Our responses and grades should nurture" (1987). Assessment in reading should focus on bringing kids along—on showing them the steps that will lead them into the reading zone, and on providing the support they'll need to sustain the journey.

> *Assessment in reading should focus on bringing kids along—on showing them the steps that will lead them into the reading zone, and on providing the support they'll need to sustain the journey.*

Communicating With Parents

Every teacher of reading needs to build a team of adults who care about books, reading, and the child as a reader. A good way to start is by sharing information about *why* parents should care. The newsletter that appears on the pages that follow goes home to every CTL family every fall. It explains why reading matters, what we do at school to teach it, and how parents can help readers, especially young ones, at home. I invite like-minded teachers to reproduce it, send it home to the parents of your students, and launch a partnership with them as grown-ups who nurture readers.

Reading
HOW PARENTS CAN HELP

A Parent Newsletter by Nancie Atwell

Everyone Has Reading Homework Every Day

The teachers at our school are committed to helping students establish the habits of readers and a lifelong love of books. Each afternoon every child leaves school with one or more books to be read at home for at least a half an hour and returned to school the next day. Depending on his or her age, your child may read to or with an adult or sibling, listen to the book read aloud, or read independently. The K–4 overnight bookbag, our gift for the year, is a demonstration of the school's commitment to children's reading.

There is no more important homework than reading. Research shows that the highest-achieving students are those who devote leisure time to reading, even when the school day and year are only mid-length. Every major study, including results from the PISA (international reading scores), the NAEP (the U.S.), and the SAT, show that the single most important predictor of academic success is the amount of time children spend reading books, more important even than parents' economic or social status. In addition, one of the few predictors of high achievement in math and science is the amount of time children devote to pleasure reading. And in a recent study, people who read literary fiction were shown to be more empathetic toward others.

Children read in order to become smarter about the world and how it works. They read to broaden their vocabularies and become better at reading—faster and more accurate, purposeful, engaged, critical, and satisfied. They read to stretch their imaginations and live vicariously with other people, in other times and places. And they read to become good people—knowledgeable about and compassionate toward a range of human experience.

There is no substitute for regular, sustained time with books. Please sit down with your child tonight and talk about the best time and place for reading to happen at your house. Is after school or before dinner a good point to curl up with a book and get lost in a great story? Or will your child join the book lovers who like to read themselves to sleep at night? And whenever reading happens, is the environment quiet? Is the TV off? Is there a good light? We've learned that the choices of books available to kids today are so wonderful that reading makes for joyful homework. We've also seen that children whose parents and teachers expect and encourage them to read books are the ones most likely to become readers.

Tips for Parents of Beginning Readers

The following are suggestions of different ways parents can support primary-grade readers. These are enjoyable, successful approaches that we use at school with our youngest students.

- Read aloud frequently from easy picture books that your child would like to read but can't yet. Sit side by side, so you can look at the pages together. Point to words occasionally or underline them with your finger as you read. Pause and make room for your child's predictions, questions, and comments about the story, characters, illustrations, and language.

- Anticipate that your child will want to hear the same books again and again. Take advantage of their love of a particular story by trying to read it as many times as you're asked, even if you're groaning inside. These are often the first stories children will read on their own.

- When you read aloud, leave an occasional blank with your voice on words or phrases you think your child can guess at. Discuss the reasons for his or her predictions. Is it a clue like beginning letter sounds, the size and shape of the word, illustrations, or common sense within a sentence or the meaning of the story?

- Read a bit aloud—a phrase or sentence— while underlining the words with your finger. Then ask your child to read it back to you, like an echo, and to underline it with his or her finger. Say, "Touch the words with your eyes" or "Read it with your finger."

- When beginning readers are reciting a book they've memorized, ask them to *touch the words* as they say them. Draw your child's attention to left-to-right structures, words, and the spaces between words. Say, "Read it with your finger." Then ask questions: "Did it match? Did you have enough words? Did you run out?"

- Encourage a child who's beginning to read to choose and reread books that he or she finds easy. In a bookstore or library, look for books like those your child brings home from school, with a strong match between the words and the illustration and with just one sentence or phrase per page.

- Take turns: you read a sentence aloud, and then your child does.

- Beginning readers sometimes substitute a word that doesn't make sense—or even sound like English. Try to bite your tongue and give them enough time to hear the mistake and correct it themselves. If they don't hear it, wait until the end, and then gently question, "Did that make sense to you?" or "You read _____," repeating exactly what was read. "Does that sound right?" Then say, "Try that again and think what might make sense."

- When your child is reading aloud with you and comes to a word he or she doesn't know, talk about its beginning sounds and its shape. Then tell your child, "Go back to the start of the sentence and get your mouth ready" to provide the word that begins with the letter[s] in question. Have him or her try the whole sentence again. It's wonderful how often children can put together all the important clues—structure of the sentence, meaning of the sentence, letters, sounds, and shape—and read the word the next time through.

- If your child can't figure out a word or doesn't have a guess, by all means, go ahead and tell what it is.

- Encourage and praise a beginning reader's self-corrections and guesses.

- When your child wants to read a book aloud to you or someone else in the family, recognize that hardly anyone reads anything perfectly the first time through. This is called "miscuing," and although everybody does it, including parents and teachers, it can be frustrating to beginning readers to make a lot of miscues. Help your child practice alone first. Then, when he or she reads aloud, encourage normal phrasing and reading for meaning: "Read it as if you're talking."

- Spend a short time hearing your child read aloud. Stop before he or she gets tired.

- The most important thing you can do, besides reading books to and with children, is to talk with them about the books. The benefits come not from sounding out words or naming letters together but from a parent asking and a child answering questions that arise naturally from a story: "What do you think about _____? How did that make you feel? What do you think's going to happen next? Who's your favorite character? What was your favorite part? Does that remind you of the time we _____? How would you compare this one to the other books by _____ or about ____?" Concentrate on your child's *feelings, preferences, opinions*, and *connections with his or her real life*.

- Try not to display anxiety or frustration. Lots of practice and relaxed, happy experiences with books are two keys to children becoming fluent, habitual readers.

Three Kinds of Books

The books that children take home at night to read or hear read aloud fall into three categories of difficulty. Leslie Funkhouser, a teacher in New Hampshire, defined the distinctions we make among books. *Holidays* are easy first reads or old favorites: a book a child has read many times or one he or she picked up to take a break from harder books. *Just Rights* are new books that help a reader practice and gain experience; they contain just a few words per page that the child doesn't know yet. *Challenges* are titles a child would like to read independently but are too difficult right now. There may be too many unfamiliar words, paragraphs that are too long, a plot or structure that's difficult to follow, multiple main characters, or concepts the child can't grasp yet.

We appreciate these definitions because they label books, not students. All readers of every age have our own Holidays, Just Rights, and Challenges. Often, as we learn more about a subject, work with a particular book, or gain more experience as a reader, a Challenge can become a Just Right. At school we watch as beginning readers make so much progress over the course of a year that a title they could only listen to in September becomes—over time and with practice—a book they read in June with fluency and understanding.

Children should spend some time at home with all three categories of books, but *most* of their time should be spent with Just Rights, because these are the books that help students learn the most about reading, what reading is good for, and the topics they're reading about.

Some time should be spent with Holidays, to help children feel confident, increase their reading rate, revisit old friends, and read for pure pleasure.

Finally, children should spend a little time with Challenges, because these often tell stories or contain information that children want and can figure out with our help, and because they show students the books that are out there waiting for them.

When your child reads—silently, to you, or with you—ask about the difficulty of the book. Is it a Holiday? A Just Right? A Challenge? Sometimes with a Just Right, and always with a Challenge, be ready to provide help with unfamiliar words or concepts. Again, bear in mind that readers shouldn't spend all their time with just one kind of book. Children need experience with materials of varying degrees of difficulty if they are to grow to independence as readers.

Reading Aloud

Please don't ever consider your child too old to be read to. At school we read aloud to our students straight through eighth grade. Children of every age cherish the literary worlds that adults bring to life with our voices. The bonds of closeness created when a grown-up and a child enjoy a story together are one of the best things about being a parent, or having one. Strickland Gillilan's poem "The Reading Mother" ends with a stanza we think gets it right: family read-alouds are a treasure.

You may have tangible wealth untold—
caskets of jewels and coffers of gold.
Richer than I you can never be.
I had a mother who read to me.

When you read stories aloud to younger children, it's helpful if you can select books from all three categories of difficulty, not just Challenges or chapter books. Feel free in your family to enjoy different kinds of stories and good writing.

Birthday Books

The teachers are grateful to parents for your support of our classroom libraries through your participation in the school's birthday book program. You and your child are invited to select and purchase a new book, paper- or hardback, to present to the classroom library on his or her birthday. Birthday bookplates are available from the teachers, as are all-purpose bookplates to commemorate other book-giving occasions, like a new title in a series or by a class favorite author.

Final Thoughts

Your child may select an overnight book with content or themes that you question. While we think it's important that children choose what they read, we also believe that your values matter. If a book bothers you and you feel strongly about it, ask your child not to bring it home again, explain why, and call his or her teacher. The teachers have selected books for our libraries with many criteria in mind, from classic literature to predictable language and story structures to award-winning illustrations to cross-cultural themes to contemporary social issues to rich information. We are always happy to explain the merits we find in a particular title. But we also want to support you if you have concerns about a book choice, and we'll help your child make a new, more appropriate one.

Because we use children's and young adult literature to teach reading, we count on our books being available at school. And because our collection of books represents a substantial investment of school funds and teachers' own money, we're discouraged when books disappear for weeks at a time or don't reappear ever. Could you help us by checking the bookbag or backpack each morning to be certain that your child has a book to return, or to continue to read that day at school? And please scour your children's bedrooms from time to time for titles that belong to the school or one of the teachers. Thanks.

Finally, please ensure that your children don't "take a break" from reading during school vacations. Research shows that the reading levels of students who stop reading during the summer drop an average of three months. Perhaps even more unsettling, the I.Q.s of children who don't read over the summer drop or stagnate, too. Frequent, enjoyable, year-round experiences with books are key.

This newsletter about reading is, admittedly, lengthy. Reading is a priority activity at our school. We know that nothing is more important to the development of children's abilities in every subject than reading and being read to.

From the first day of school, we make time for looking at books, listening to books, talking about the ideas and people in books, learning how to read books, and reading them. We offer students the most generous invitations we can devise to help them fall in love with books, see themselves as readers, spend time practicing, and become fluent and accurate. We know that the richness of their early experiences as readers will serve them well their whole lifetimes, and we look forward to partnering with you as grown-ups who nurture readers.

Summer Reading Loss

As I mentioned, in the reading newsletter, summer reading loss, which is also called *summer slide* or *summer setback*, is a concerning phenomenon. Children who live in urban areas that researchers Neuman and Moland (2016) describe as "book deserts," along with our own students who live in rural isolation in towns without libraries or bookstores, don't read in the summer. In September, they return to the classroom three months behind where they were in June (Cooper, et al., 1996). Children without access to books slide further backward every summer. As Richard Allington describes it, "The accumulating effect…means that poor children during their elementary school years may fall as much as two years behind more advantaged students, even if the instruction during the school year produced identical reading growth in both groups" (2012).

But there's good news. A study conducted by Allington and McGill-Franzen (2013) shows that given a dozen story books of their own choosing to read over the summer and to keep as their own, children from high-poverty settings not only maintained their skills, they made reading gains as great as those associated with having attended summer school. Even so, Allington observes, "Hardly any schools send poor kids home with a supply of books to read in the summer."

The CTL faculty decided not to differentiate between poor kids and those from better-off families but to send every student home every June with a supply of books to read over the summer. A local supermarket donated reusable bags in support of the effort, and our kids fill them up. They peruse classroom libraries and choose the books they want to borrow, typically at least a half dozen in grades 5–8 and lots more in K–4. They sign out the books on index cards, which their teachers photocopy. We staple the copies to the summer bookbags, file the originals at school, and in September check the books back into our libraries. Since 2009, the grades 7–8 book collection has lost a grand total of four titles to summer readers—worth it, since every student participated in "the single summer activity that is most strongly and consistently related to summer learning" (Heyns, 1978) *and* lived inside some great stories in the process.

On the first day of school, readers return their summer books

This is a reading teacher's best and lasting legacy. We are the ones who built the bridge and guided kids into the reading zone.

A Worthwhile Legacy

Reading workshop is a great place for kids to practice comprehension, build accuracy and stamina, acquire vocabulary, and develop critical eyes and ears. But above all, reading workshop is the bridge. Children cross over it from the drabness of a world bereft of stories to one that's healthy, multidimensional, fully alive, delight filled, and sustaining. The people and ideas they encounter here, the vicarious adventures they live here, can only be found in books. This is a reading teacher's best and lasting legacy. We are the ones who built the bridge and guided kids into the reading zone.

What We Talk About When We Talk About Poetry: A Lexicon

alliteration – the repetition of beginning sounds, usually consonants, in neighboring words

allegory – a story with a second meaning hidden inside its literal one

allusion – within a poem, a reference to a literary work or an event, person, or place outside of the poem

anaphora – repetition in which the same word or phrase is repeated, often at the beginning of lines

anastrophe – a deliberate inversion of the normal order of words

annotation – a reader's comments written on a poem

anthology – a book of poems by different poets

assonance – the repetition of vowel sounds in neighboring words

cadence– a rhythmic pattern that's based on the natural repetitions and emphases in speech

caesura (si·ZHOOR·uh) – a slight but definite pause *inside* a line of a poem created by the rhythm of the language or a punctuation mark, e.g., a period, dash, or colon in the middle of a line

cliché – an expression that has been used so often it has lost its freshness or meaning, e.g., a rainbow of colors, as busy as a bee, a blanket of snow; note: the adjective form is *clichéd*

close form – poetry written to an established pattern, e.g., a sonnet, limerick, villanelle, pantoum, tritina, sestina, or rondel

collection – a book of poems by one poet

concrete – a real, tangible detail or example of something; opposite of *abstract* or *general*

couplet – a pair of lines, usually written in the same form

connotation – the emotions and associations that a word suggests beyond its literal meaning

denotation – the literal or dictionary meaning of a word

diction – a poet's word choices

elegy – a poem of mourning or praise for the dead

end-stopped line – when meaning *and* grammar pause at the end of a line; a line-break at a normal pause in speech, usually at a punctuation mark; the opposite of an *enjambed line* or *enjambment*

enjambed line – when the meaning and grammar of a line continue from one line to the next with no pause; also called a *run-on line*

epigraph – a quotation placed at the beginning of a poem to make the theme more resonant

figurative language – comparisons between unrelated things or ideas: metaphor, simile, personification, and hyperbole are all types of figurative language, which reveals the familiar in new, surprising ways; the opposite of *literal language*

free verse – poetry that doesn't have a set rhythm, line length, or rhyme scheme; instead, it relies on the natural rhythms of speech; today the most widely practiced kind of poetry in the English language

form – the structure of a poem; how it is built

hyperbole – when a poet exaggerates on purpose for effect

image/imagery – a sensory response evoked in the mind of a reader by the diction in a poem; not just visual but any sensory impression—sound, touch, taste, odor—inspired by language

irony – when a poet says one thing but means something else

line – a group of words in a row; the unit of a poem

line break – the most important point in a line of poetry: the pause or breath at the end of a line

literal language – the straightforward meanings of words; the opposite of *figurative language*

lyric poetry – short poems (fewer than sixty lines) about personal experiences or feelings; most verse written today is lyric poetry

metaphor – a comparison in which the poet writes about one thing as if it is something else: A = B, with the qualities of B transferred to A

open form – see *free verse*

oxymoron – a figure of speech that combines two words that contradict each other, e.g., bittersweet

personification – a comparison that gives human qualities to an object, animal, idea, or phenomenon

poet laureate – a title given to an outstanding U.S. poet by the Library of Congress, usually for one or two years

prose poem – a piece of writing that has poetic features—rhythm, imagery, compression—but doesn't rhyme, conform to a set rhythm, or break into lines

rhyme scheme – the pattern of rhyming in a poem; to describe the pattern, each line is assigned a letter, and lines that rhyme are given the same letter, e.g., abab

sensory diction – language in a poem that evokes one of the five senses

simile – a kind of metaphor that uses *like* or *as* to compare two things: A is like B

speaker/persona – the voice that speaks the words of a poem, not necessarily the same person as the poet

stanza – a line or group of lines in a poem separated from other lines by extra white space; a division in a poem that occurs at a natural pause or at a point where the poet wants to speed up or slow down the poem, shift its tone, change the setting, or introduce a new idea or character

symbol – a thing or action that represents something else in addition to itself

tercet – a unit of three lines, usually written in the same form

theme – an idea about life that emerges from a poem

tone – the attitude of the speaker or poet toward the subject of the poem or its reader

tricolon – a rhythm, pattern, or emphasis used three times; a.k.a. "the power of three"

turn – a point in a poem when the meaning moves in a new, significant direction, or its theme emerges

What We Talk About When We Talk About Stories: A Lexicon

action – the events of the story; what the characters do

allegory – a story with a second meaning hidden inside its literal one

allusion – within a story, a reference to a literary work or an event, person, or place outside of the story

ambiguous – uncertain; open to different interpretations

annotation – a reader's written comments on a text

antagonist – the character who most strongly opposes the hero or heroine in a conflict; opposite of *protagonist*

anti-hero – a main character without the admirable qualities of a typical hero

atmosphere – the feelings a reader gets from a story based on its details, usually those related to its setting

attitude – see *tone*

black comedy – a story that makes light of a serious subject, such as death or war

cadence – a rhythmic pattern that's based on the natural rhythms, repetitions, and emphases in speech

caricature – a character who is exaggerated or unconvincing as a real person

catharsis – an outpouring of emotion, usually at the end of a story

character – a person in a story

character development – the way an author describes the people in a story—their actions, speech, and thoughts

cliché – an expression that has been used so often it has lost its freshness or meaning, e.g., a rainbow of colors, as busy as a bee, a blanket of snow; note: the adjective form is *clichéd*

climax – the point in a story when the plot reaches its highest point of intensity

coherent – writing that sticks together, that's consistent and doesn't contradict itself

comic relief – a humorous element in a story that's otherwise dramatic; usually used to relieve tension or draw a contrast

concrete – a real, tangible detail or example of something; opposite of *abstract* or *general*

conflict – the opposition of two characters or forces; the classic conflicts found in literature are person against person, person against society, people against nature, and an individual against him- or herself

consistent – a plot event or a character's actions that agree with what has already happened in the story

copyright page – in a book, the page after the title page; it tells a reader who holds the rights to a book (usually the author), when it was first published, when it was published as a paperback, the name and address of the publisher(s), the Library of Congress number and ISBN for the book, and the number of times it had been reprinted so far, i.e., how well it has sold

denouement – the resolution or clearing up of the complications of a plot, found at the conclusion

deus ex machina – an improbable or contrived ending; translates to "god from the machine," a device that was lowered onto the stage at the end of Greek plays to provide a tidy conclusion

dialogue – the words spoken among characters

diction – an author's word choices

dystopian literature – a pessimistic depiction of life in the future

edition – a printed version of a book that's distinguished from its other versions either in form (paperback vs. hardback) or content (first edition vs. second)

epigraph – a quotation placed at the beginning of a piece of writing to make the theme more resonant

epilogue – a final section of a story that explains what happens after the main events

epistolary novel – a story told through letters or emails

flashback – a scene that returns to an earlier time

flashforward – a scene that moves ahead in time

flat character – a person who is simple, predictable, and doesn't change over the course of a story (E. M. Forster); opposite of *round character*

foreshadowing – when an author hints at what's to come in a story

format – the structure of a book

formula/formulaic – a piece of writing in which the plot or format is so familiar, has been used so often, that the writing is stale and predictable

genre – a type of literature

hero – a main character with admirable qualities

image/imagery – a sensory response produced in the mind of a reader; not just mental pictures but any sensory impression evoked by language

intention – purpose

interior monologue – a sustained description of a character's thoughts, written as though overheard directly from his or her mind

irony – when an author says one thing but means something else

marginalia – notes a reader writes in the margins of a book

meta- – a work that comments on its own status; in metafiction, the author directly addresses the conventions of fiction and acknowledges that this piece of writing is a part of them

mixed review – a critique that includes both positive and negative comments

motif – an event, situation, theme, character, or pattern that shows up in many literary works

motivation – the reasons behind a character's actions; usually a combination of personality and situation

narrative – a true or fictional account of a series of events; a story

narrator – the voice that tells the story; see *point of view*

nom de plume – "pen name"; a name used by a writer instead of his or her real name

novella – a fictional story that, in length, falls between a short story and a novel

oeuvre – the works of an author taken all together

pace – the speed at which a story unfolds

pan – a negative review

paradox – a statement that contradicts itself although it appears to be true

persona – a character taken on by an author to narrate a story

perspective – the position from which a story's events are observed

plausible – appearing to be true or realistic

plot – the events in a story

plot device – something used by an author to move the story forward, usually an object, event, or character

point of view – the position from which the narrator observes the events of a story; first-person (I), second person (you), third person (he or she), omniscient (can see everyone's perspective), and limited omniscient (can see the thoughts and feelings of selected characters); also see *unreliable narrator*

post-apocalyptic literature – fiction set in a world or civilization after its destruction

premise – an idea that provides the basis of a plot

prologue – an introduction to a literary work

prose – writing that isn't poetry; the ordinary form of written language

protagonist – the main character in a story; opposite of *antagonist*

pseudonym – a "false name" used by an author

quartet – a set of four books

rave – an enthusiastic positive review

realism – a true-to-life representation of a person or situation

reflections – the thoughts and feelings of a character

resolution – the part of a plot where the conflict is worked out, usually at the end of a story

roman a clef – a "novel with a key": a story in which real people, thinly disguised, appear under fictional names

round character – a complex, dynamic person who changes over the course of a story (E. M. Forster); opposite of *flat character*

scene – one episode in a story

sensory details – descriptions that evoke one or more of the five senses: visual (sight), olfactory (smell), auditory (sound), tactile (touch), and gustatory (taste)

sequel – a book that continues the story of a previous book

series – a group of novels related by plot, characters, and/or setting

setting – the time and place in which a story occurs

stereotype – a too-simple, standardized idea about all the members of one group

stream of consciousness – a character's thoughts written in a realistic, continuous flow

style – the way an author uses words; how an author's diction, syntax, tone, punctuation, etc., work together in a story

suspend disbelief – put aside logic in order to enjoy a story

symbol – an object or action that represents a larger meaning

tense – the time in which the action takes place: past, present, or future

tension – a situation in a story that gives the reader a strong sense of worry, uncertainty, or fear

theme – an idea about life that emerges from a story

tone – the attitude the author takes toward his or her subject or audience

trilogy – a set of three books by one author

unreliable narrator – the voice telling a story when it doesn't understand or know the truth, or is withholding it on purpose

utopian literature – a story set in an imagined perfect society

vignette – a very short story focused on one moment

Appendix C

How to Create a National Reading Zone

1. Acknowledge that poverty, not poor teaching or a lack of standards, is the central issue affecting student achievement in reading in the United States. For the first time in recent history, a majority of public school students fall below the federal low-income cutoff. All of our kids need *books*, they need them early, and they need them year-round.

> *Ensure that every child has easy access to terrific books to read voluntarily. Poor children have fewer books in their schools, fewer books in the stores in their neighborhoods, and fewer children's books in the public libraries that serve their communities. Fewer books than middle-class kids on each count. It is time to ensure that we eliminate the "book deserts" that so many poor children live in.*
>
> —**Richard Allington**

> *High levels of poverty are associated with lower reading achievement. There is good reason for this: Lack of access to reading material is associated with lower test scores. If we invest more in libraries and librarians, the entire country could become a reading zone despite the presence of poverty.*
>
> —**Stephen Krashen**

> *Close the summer literacy gap by offering all children, no matter their zip code, quality summer reading experiences with books and the joys of reading. At the city and local level, deliver books to children's homes at every key moment, from birth to the start of kindergarten and onward. Advocate for equity in publishing: make sure diverse texts that represent a wide range of children's lives get published and stay published. And we must champion access to broadband Internet in every neighborhood so all our nation's children can become readers of digital text.*
>
> —**Pam Allyn**

> *Work with the Departments of Juvenile Justice to stock libraries and provide access to books to the tens of thousands of youth who are held in juvenile facilities on any given day in the U.S. In addition, colleges, universities, and other agencies need to establish community-based reading clinics and provide outreach to advance the reading development of children and adolescents.*
>
> —**Alfred Tatum**

2. The federal and state governments need to earmark funds for the purchase of children's and young adult literature for K–12 classroom and school libraries, with a goal of at least twenty titles per student.

3. Foundations and the charitable arms of corporations that care about children's lives and literacy can underwrite massive purchases of trade books for distribution in low-income communities and donation to classroom and school libraries.

4. Teachers and parents can lobby administrators and school boards to budget funds for teachers and librarians to invest in trade books instead of purchasing expensive core reading programs that waste money and class time.

5. School administrators can develop systems that make it easy for classroom teachers to select and purchase trade books one title at a time and *not* without reimbursement.

6. Trade publishers can give schools and libraries a healthy discount on children's and young adult literature—30–40% off list prices.

7. Teachers of independent readers can establish a network of websites of great titles nominated by K–12 students from diverse communities: the favorites of all kinds of kids as a go-to resource for selecting books that students will read with pleasure.

8. Parents of teenagers can band together, meet with high school English departments, and ask that their almost-adult children be trusted and allowed to read for pleasure as their summer assignment—and, during the school year, choose many of their own books, read a lot, discover their reading preferences, and develop the habits of lifelong readers.

9. Professional organizations dedicated to literacy and literature must *take a stand* against instruction, standards, and standardized tests that stunt children's growth as readers; they can also disseminate research findings for teachers to cite in support of voluminous independent reading—see Scholastic's research compendium (Bridges, 2016) as a model.

10. Teachers need to act as professionals and reflective practitioners, not be reduced to mere technicians who tinker with unproven, standardized practices. We must fight against mandates that deny students their own choices of books and the time they need to read them. How to take action?

- Read the relevant research, and if challenged, cite it.

- Close our doors, observe our students, and develop reading workshops that support their activity and growth as independent readers. Collect and share data: numbers of books, range of genres, and such pre- and post-workshop assessment results as documentation of the levels of books students can read independently in September as compared to June.

- Establish study groups in our schools or districts that include as many administrators as we can convince to join us. Read and discuss articles that tell the truth about reading development and the most effective instruction—start with "Every Child, Every Day" by Richard Allington and Rachael Gabriel (2012).

- Inform legislators about the on-the-ground impacts of mandated curricula and standardized tests. Program their phone numbers and email addresses into our cellphones and, at the end of every bad day, leave or text a message that describes what our kids had to endure that day *and* what they never got to experience as readers because of baseless standards, misguided methods, and the overabundance of test-prep activities. Bombard those in positions of power with our stories about the effects of their policies.

Teachers can resist, rather than reflexively comply with, any curriculum standards imposed on us that threaten the reading zones we've created in our classrooms. This includes the Common Core, with its disproportionate emphasis on informational texts, its diminution of students' interpretations and prior experiences, and its emphasis on test preparation.

—Alfie Kohn

11. The whole community of people who care about literacy can ask of U.S. classrooms: Where are the real books? Where is the time to read them? Where is evidence of the voluminous research that shows that students achieve reading proficiency only through reading?

References

Allington, R., McGill-Franzen, A., Camilli, G., Williams, L., Graff, J., Zeig, J., & Nowak, R. (2010). Addressing summer setback among economically disadvantaged elementary students. *Reading Psychology, 31*, 411–427.

Allington, R., & Gabriel, R. (2012). Every child, every day. *Educational Leadership, 69* (6), 10–15.

Allington, R. (2012). *What really matters for struggling readers.* New York: Addison Wesley.

Allington, R., & McGill-Franzen, A. (2013). *Summer reading: Closing the rich/poor achievement gap.* New York: Teachers College Press.

Atwell, N. (2002). *Lessons that change writers.* Portsmouth, NH: Heinemann.

Atwell, N. (2006). *Naming the world: A year of poems and lessons.* Portsmouth, NH: Heinemann.

Atwell, N. (2007). *The reading zone (1st ed.).* New York: Scholastic.

Atwell, N. (2014). *Systems to transform your classroom and school.* Portsmouth, NH: Heinemann.

Atwell, N. (2015). *In the middle (3rd edition).* Portsmouth, NH: Heinemann.

Baldwin, J. (1963). Doom and glory of knowing who you are. Interview by Jane Howard. *Life Magazine, 54* (21), 89.

Bridges, L. (2016). *A summary of research and expert opinion on the joy and power of reading.* Scholastic Research Compendium, scholastic.com.

Bruner, J. (1986). *Actual minds, possible worlds.* Cambridge, MA: Harvard University Press.

Bureau of Labor Statistics (2015). U.S. Department of Labor, *The Economics Daily,* Time spent in leisure activities in 2014 by gender, age, and educational attainment.

Coffin, H. (2009). *Every child a reader: Month-by-month lessons to teach beginning reading.* New York: Scholastic.

Coleman, D., and Pimentel, S. (2012). Revised publishers' criteria for the Common Core State Standards in English language arts and literacy, grades 3–12. Common Core State Standards Initiative. NGA Center/CCSSO, 12 Apr. 2012. Web. 28. July 2012.

Collins, B. (1996). Introduction to poetry. *The apple that astonished Paris.* Faytetteville, AR: University of Arkansas Press.

The Common Core State Standards Initiative (2011). Available at www.corestandards.org/read-the-standards/.

Common Sense Media (2014). *Children, teens, and reading.* commonsensemedia.org.

Cooper, H., Nye, B., Charlton, K., Lindsay, J., & Greathouse, S. (1996). The effects of summer vacation on achievement test scores: A narrative meta-analytic review. *Review of Educational Research, 66,* 227–268.

Cunningham, A., & Zibulsky, J. (2014). *Book smart: How to develop and support successful, motivated readers.* New York: Oxford University Press.

Davies, R. (1959). Battle cry for book lovers. *The Saturday Evening Post.* Expanded and reprinted in *A voice from the attic,* 1960. New York: Knopf.

Ehri, L. C., Dreyer, L. G., Flugman, B., & Gross, A. (2007). Reading rescue: An effective tutoring intervention model for language minority students who are struggling readers in first grade. *American Educational Research Journal, 44* (2), 414–448.

Eldredge, J. L. (1995). *Teaching decoding in holistic classrooms.* Englewood Cliffs, NJ: Prentice-Hall.

Fair, D. A., Cohen, A. L., Powers, J., Dosenbach, N., Church, J., Miezen, F., Schlagger, B., & Peterson, S. (2009). Functional brain networks develop from a local to a distributed organization. *PLoS Computational Biology, 5* (5).

Gallagher, K. (2015). *In the best interests of students.* Portland, ME: Stenhouse.

Gallagher, K. (2009). *Readicide.* Portland, ME: Stenhouse.

Graham, S., & Herbert, M. (2010). Writing to read: A meta-analysis of the impact of writing and writing instruction on reading. *Harvard Educational Review. Vol. 81.* No. 4 Winter.

Graves, D. (1983). *Writing: Teachers & children at work.* Portsmouth, NH: Heinemann.

Greene, G. (1940). *The power and the glory.* London: Heinemann.

Guthrie, J. T., & Humenick, N. M. (2004). Motivating students to read: Evidence for classroom practices that increase motivation and achievement. In P. McCardle & V. Chhabra (Eds.), *The voice of evidence in reading research* (pp. 329–354). Baltimore: Paul Brookes.

Hakim, J. (1993–2005). *A history of US.* New York: Oxford University Press.

Hansen, J. (1987). *When writers read.* Portsmouth, NH: Heinemann.

Harvey, S., and Danielson, H. (2009). *Comprehension and collaboration.* Portsmouth, NH: Heinemann.

Harwayne, S. (1992). *Lasting impressions: Weaving literature into the writing workshop.* Portsmouth, NH: Heinemann.

Heyns, B. (1978). *Summer learning and the effects of schooling.* New York: Academic Press.

Hiebert, E., & Reutzel, R. (2010). *Revisiting silent reading: New directions for teachers and researchers.* Newark, DE: International Literacy Association.

Howells, W. D. (1902). *Literature and life.* New York: Harper and Brothers.

Kassin, S. M., and Lepper, M. R. (1984). Oversufficient and insufficient justification effects: Cognitive behavioral development. In J. Nicholls (Ed.), *The development of achievement motivation.* Greenwich, CT: JAI Press.

Kidd, D., & Castano, E. (2013). Reading literary fiction improves theory of mind. *Science, 342* (6156), 377–380.

Kids and Family Reading Report (2007). Commissioned by Scholastic: conducted by Yankelovich. Retrieved from www.scholastic.com/aboutscholastic/news/readingreport.htm.

Kirby, D. L. (2016). Reading and writing relationships: Narratives as the core of the English classroom. *English Journal,* January, 43–48.

Kittle, P. (2013). *Book love.* Portsmouth, NH: Heinemann.

Kohn, Alfie (2015). A dozen essential guidelines for educators. In *Schooling beyond measure.* Portsmouth, NH: Heinemann.

Krashen, S. (2011). *Free voluntary reading.* Santa Barbara, CA: Unlimited Libraries.

LeGuin, U. (1970). Prophets and mirrors: Science fiction as a way of seeing. *The Living Light 7* (3), Fall, 1970.

Magill, F. N. (Ed.). (1991). *Masterpieces of world literature in digest form.* New York: HarperCollins.

Mangen, A., Walgermo, B., & Bronnick, K. (2013). Reading linear texts on paper versus computer screen: Effects on reading comprehension. *International Journal of Educational Research, Vol. 58,* 61–68.

Mangen, A., Robinet, P., Olivier, G., & Velay, J. L. (July, 2014). *Mystery story reading in pocket print book and on kindle: Possible impact on chronological events memory.* IGEL: International Society for the Empirical Study of Literature and Media Conference.

Marinak, B. (2003). What sustains engagement in reading? Presentation at the National Reading Conference, Phoenix, AZ (December, 2003).

McCann, C. (2015). *Thirteen ways of looking.* New York: Random House.

Meck, M. (1982). *Learning to read.* London: Bodley Head.

McQuillan, J. (1997). The effects of incentives on reading. *Reading Research and Instruction, 36,* 111–125.

Morgan, A., Wilcox, B., & Eldredge, L. (2000). Effect of difficulty levels on second-grade delayed readers using dyad reading. *The Journal of Educational Research, 94,* 113–119.

Murphy, B. (Ed.) (1996). *Benét's reader's encyclopedia* (4th ed.). New York: HarperCollins.

The nation's report card: Reading (2011). Washington, DC: National Center for Education Statistics, Institute of Education Sciences, U.S. Department of Education.

Neuman, S., and Moland, N. (2016). Book deserts: The consequences of income segregation on children's access to print. *Urban Education,* 1–22.

Newkirk, T. (1991). The middle class and the problem of pleasure. In N. Atwell (Ed.) *Workshop 3: The politics of process.* Portsmouth, NH: Heinemann.

Newkirk, T. (2000). Literacy and loneliness. *Ohio Journal of the English Language Arts.* Fall, 2000, 18–21.

Newkirk, T. (2014). *Minds made for stories: How we really read and write informational and persuasive texts.* Portsmouth, NH: Heinemann.

Newkirk, T. (2016). Unbalanced literacy: Reflections on the common core. *Language Arts, 93* (4).

Padgett, R. (1987). *The teachers and writers handbook of poetic forms.* New York: Teachers and Writers.

Pennac, D. (1994). *Better than life.* Toronto, Ontario: Coach House Press.

Prose, F. (2016, February 20). Is it harder to be transported by a book as you get older? *New York Times Book Review.*

Pruzinsky, T. (2014). Read books. Every day. Mostly for pleasure. *English Journal, 103* (4), 25–30.

Pullman, P. (2005, January 22). Common sense has much to learn from moonshine. *The Guardian.*

Rich, A. (1971). Images for godard. *The will to change.* New York: W.W. Norton and Company.

Romano, T. (1987). *Clearing the way: Working with teenage writers.* Portsmouth, NH: Heinemann.

Rosenblatt, L. M. (1978/1994). *The reader, the text, the poem: The transactional theory of the literary work* (rev. ed.). Carbondale, IL: Southern Illinois University Press.

Rosenblatt, L. M. (1938/1995). *Literature as exploration (fifth ed.)*. New York: Modern Language Association.

Sewell, E. (2003). *Students' choice of books during self-selected reading*. EDRS opinion papers.

Smith, F. (1997). *Reading without nonsense*. New York: Teachers College Press.

Smith, F. (1983). *Essays into literacy*. Portsmouth, NH: Heinemann.

Snow, C. (2013). Cold versus warm close reading: Stamina and the accumulation of misdirection. *Literacy Daily* (June 6).

Spufford, E. (2002). *The child that books built*. London: Faber and Faber.

Stafford, W. (1998). Notice what this poem is not doing. *The way it is: New & selected poems*. St. Paul, MN: Greywolf Press.

Stanovich, K., and Cunningham, A. (1993). Where does knowledge come from? Specific associations between print exposure and information acquisition. *Journal of Educational Psychology*, 85(2): 211–229.

Staton, J. (1980). Writing and counseling: Using a dialogue journal. *Language Arts*, 57, 514–518.

Steinem, G. (2015). *My life on the road*. New York: Random House.

Stevens, W. (1951). The noble rider and the sound of words. In *The necessary angel: Essays on reality and imagination*. New York: Alfred A. Knopf.

Sullivan, A., & Brown, M. (2013). *Social inequalities in cognitive scores at age 16: The role of reading*. London: Centre for Longitudinal Studies.

Thomas, D. (1952). *A few words of a kind*. Cambridge, MA: Lecture at the Massachusetts Institute of Technology.

Trelease, J. (2013). *The read-aloud handbook (7th ed.)*. New York: Penguin.

Turner, M. (1996). *The literary mind*. New York: Oxford University Press.

Veatch, J. (1968). *How to teach reading with children's books*. New York: Richard C. Owen Publishers.

Vygotsky, L. S. (1978). *Mind in society: The development of higher psychological processes*. Cambridge, MA: Harvard University Press.

West, R., and Stanovich, K. (1991). The incidental acquisition of information from reading. *Psychological Science* 2: 325–330.

West, R., Stanovich, K., and Mitchell, H. (1993). Reading in the real world and its correlates. *Reading Research Quarterly* 28: 35–50.

Wilde, O. (1891/2011). *The picture of Dorian Gray (preface)*. Cambridge, MA: Belknap Press of Harvard University Press.

Wimsatt, W. K., & Beardsley, M. C. (1954). *The verbal icon: Studies in the meaning of poetry*. Lexington, KY: University Press of Kentucky.

Woolf, V. (1947). *The moment and other essays*. New York: Harcourt Brace.

Index